El día de los niños / El día de los libros

Building a Culture of Literacy
in Your Community through Día

El día de los niños / El día de los libros

Building a Culture of Literacy in Your Community through Día

Jeanette Larson
Association for Library Service to Children

American Library Association
Chicago   2011

JEANETTE LARSON has more than thirty years of library experience. She currently teaches at Texas Woman's University and is an independent trainer for libraries around the country. An active member of the Association for Library Service to Children and the Texas Library Association (TLA), Larson's involvement with El día de los niños/El día de los libros, often called Día, began early in the initiative's history, with the development of an informational booklet of program ideas. More recently, she served on a TLA committee that produced a grant-funded Día tool kit for libraries. In 2003, she served as a member of the Estela and Raúl Mora Award Committee of REFORMA, the National Association to Promote Library and Information Services to Latinos and the Spanish-Speaking. Larson has an MSLS from the University of Southern California and a BA in anthropology from the University of New Mexico. She is also the author of a children's book, *Hummingbirds: Facts and Folklore from the Americas.*

Printed in the United States of America
15 14 13 12 11   5 4 3 2 1

While extensive effort has gone into ensuring the reliability of the information in this book, the publisher makes no warranty, express or implied, with respect to the material contained herein.

ISBN: 978-0-8389-3599-6

Library of Congress Cataloging-in-Publication Data
Larson, Jeanette.
 El día de los niños/El día de los libros : building a culture of literacy in your community through Día / Jeanette Larson.
    p. cm.—(Celebrating culture in your library series)
 Includes bibliographical references and index.
 ISBN 978-0-8389-3599-6 (alk. paper)
 1. Children's libraries—Activity programs—United States. 2. Family literacy programs—United States. 3. Reading promotion—United States. 4. Multicultural education—United States. I. Title.
 Z718.3.L37 2011
 027.62'5—dc22
                                                                                    2010053869

Cover design by Patricia Galarza-Hernandez.
Book design in ITC Kabel and Charis SIL by Karen Sheets de Gracia.

♾ This paper meets the requirements of ANSI/NISO Z39.48-1992 (Permanence of Paper).

ALA Editions also publishes its books in a variety of electronic formats. For more information, visit the ALA Store at www.alastore.ala.org and select eEditions.

Contents

Foreword

I still remember the sunny day in 1996 when the idea for this celebration first came to me. The official name of what is now a national family literacy initiative is a long one: El día de los niños/El día de los libros, Children's Day/Book Day. Often referred to as simply Día, which means "day" in Spanish, the initiative promotes a daily commitment to linking all children to books, languages, and cultures. Día, then, handily and accurately conveys a yearlong goal; day by day, *día por día*, librarians, teachers, and families creatively work to foster "bookjoy." In April, hundreds of culminating celebrations are held across the country.

Día is now housed at the Association for Library Service to Children (ALSC), a division of the American Library Association. I'm grateful to the staff and members of ALSC, who work to strengthen and grow Día; to REFORMA, the National Association to Promote Library and Information Services to Latinos and the Spanish-Speaking, my first partner; and to the countless community partners throughout the United States who participate in local Día events. In this book, Texas librarian Jeanette Larson, who has been part of the Día journey from the beginning, shares Día's history, goals, and many programming suggestions.

Ideally, those working for years on any good project grow with it as together they explore the challenges and opportunities for collaborating and for increasing the impact of the project. In 1997, we worked to have the first celebrations linking children and books on April 30. Members of REFORMA were quickly ready to collaborate and plan for Día's future with me. Soon, we realized that the challenge was promoting not an annual celebration but a yearlong commitment. Although planning and implementing the April celebration requires organization and cooperation, the true Día challenge is to inspire one another and others to link all children to books, languages, and cultures throughout the year. Día has grown and grown. Today, because many large public library systems have their annual, culminating celebrations at different branches, they understandably schedule their Día celebrations on different days.

Why do we humans like celebrations such as birthdays, graduations, and anniversaries? A quick answer is that, as social creatures, we savor occasions for getting together to enjoy food and laughter even when planning and cleanup require effort. At a deeper level, celebrations are occasions to look both to the past and to the future, to ask, Where are we on the journey, are we on the right path, are we being imaginative and resourceful to deepen our potential, and are we learning from the good examples around us?

In speaking of Día, who is "we"? I've written about this little word for years—the "slippery we," I once called it in an essay. "We" is the national Día community, all who have worked on Día, who believe in its potential to honor languages and cultures, to increase literacy and a love of books in our richly multiethnic country. "We" also includes those of you who want to embrace this call to action and to engage not only your usual patrons but also the often underserved families who may find the library or school intimidating because they don't speak English or may lack familiarity with our institutions. I often quote my friends at the Charlotte Mecklenburg Library who say that Día stands for "Diversity in Action."

Not all the families we seek to reach may be reading families, and many may need us to be their enthusiastic literacy coaches, helping them to understand that families don't need to speak English to support their children's literacy journey. I wrote extensively about this in my new book, *ZING! Seven Creativity Practices for Educators and Students*, where I included the following lines:

> Together, cada día, every day,
> we're building the bridge to bookjoy.

Advocacy, supporting and championing a cause—in this example, the rights of all families to feel part of their library and school community, encouraging them to be leaders and to have their ideas heard and respected—is no small task. Advocacy work can be discouraging since bureaucracies have their structures and rules, and yet—and yet—the most impressive Día champions are those who are undaunted, who see that for our nation to remain a democracy, our citizens need to be readers and critical thinkers who can access and understand information and ideas.

When I ask winners of the annual Estela and Raúl Mora Award what their greatest challenge was, they often say, "Convincing staff to buy in to why Día is so important." Winning staff also state that it's a challenge for a library to create a truly multicultural book celebration. Jeanette Larson offers suggestions for doing so in this book. To begin, we can reflect on this question: are we modeling our rhetoric, community collaboration? Staff members are pleasantly surprised at the rewards of really reaching out and benefiting familiar and new patrons, making new friends, and creating a true community celebration of bookjoy. "It feels good!" they say, even when they're tired after the annual fiesta.

Día can be dismissed as too much of a challenge or as merely a sweet party for children and families. Far from it, my friends. Yes, the celebration day is great fun, and through the years, I've been the grateful beneficiary of the hard work of Día committees, which ideally are diverse and include an array of community members. I've particularly enjoyed the literacy activities: book walks, book making, bilingual puppet shows, book giveaways, and so on. I've also enjoyed the piñatas, mariachis, and cookies, and all kinds of other foods and music from other countries. The vibrant and playful illustrations by Rafael López in my book *Book Fiesta! Celebrate Children's Day/Book Day / Celebremos El día de los niños/El día de los libros* convey children enjoying books on an elephant, in a whale's mouth, in a submarine, in a hot-air balloon. Page after page, and for Día advocates, day after day, *día por día*, we're saying, "Reading is fun!" Come visit me at my website, www.patmora.com, where we can continue to chat about Día and its potential to change libraries and communities and to change us.

Let's return to the topic of celebrating. I wish I could host a huge party with lots of good food and clever, glittery book-related favors and invite each of you who is part of the national Día community. We'd have a moment of silence to honor Rose Treviño, Día's guardian angel, and we'd clap for Oralia Garza de Cortés, a "Día Dynamo." I'd so like to thank you all of you in person for your persistent literacy advocacy. I'd invite all the new librarians and future educators who've decided to join us, too. You are so needed! The literacy statistics in this country are grim, but we—a diverse, determined, committed group of literacy advocates—can collaborate and imaginatively reach out to families who don't know the book pleasure that we experience or who don't yet believe that our libraries are safe, welcoming, and respectful places that honor home languages and welcome all who seek to read and learn. Together, my friends, let's build the bridge to bookjoy.

PAT MORA

Acknowledgments

I've been involved with El día de los niños/El día de los libros since its infancy, and it has been my privilege along the journey to work with some wonderful and creative librarians. Regardless of their own linguistic and cultural background, they all have shared a passion for promoting reading in any language. First and foremost, I thank Pat Mora for telling me about her idea to promote bookjoy and bilingual literacy and for first asking me fifteen years ago whether I had any ideas for bringing El día de los niños/El día de los libros to the attention of librarians. I also express my thanks and appreciation to Linda Mays, program officer for projects and partnerships at the Association for Library Service to Children, for tirelessly answering my questions and for her continued dedication to El día de los niños/El día de los libros. There are many other people, like my Italian friend Rossella Pivanti, who willingly allowed me to include their material in this book and answered questions about cultural authenticity. It goes without saying that my husband, James W. Larson, also provided a lot of personal support, technical assistance, and artistic talent for the book. He had no idea what he signed on for when he married a children's librarian! Thanks also to all of the librarians and library staff members who responded to my requests for information about their programs. In some cases, the information was aggregated and is not identifiable, but in other instances, I have identified the sources of programming and other information. My appreciation goes especially to the following librarians who spent time talking to me, sent me photographs and samples, and answered my questions:

Ramarie Beaver, Plano (Texas) Public Library
Tina Birkholz, Gail Borden Public Library, Elgin, Illinois

Lida Clouser, McCall (Idaho) Public Library

Ida daRoza, San Mateo County (California) Public Library

Donna DeButts, Ypsilanti (Michigan) District Library

Oralia Garza de Cortés, Austin (Texas)

Sara Howrey, retired librarian

Meg Lojek, McCall (Idaho) Public Library

Freda Mosquera, Broward County (Florida) Library

Riann Powell, Albuquerque/Bernalillo County (New Mexico) Library System

Judy Rohr, Topeka and Shawnee County (Kansas) Library

Ana Schmitt, Multnomah County Library, Portland, Oregon

Lise Tewes, Kenton County (Kentucky) Public Library

Martha A. Toscano, El Paso (Texas) Public Library

Beatriz Pascual Wallace, Seattle (Washington) Public Library

1
What Is El día de los niños / El día de los libros?

Librarians and educators have long recognized the need for children to have great books available to them. We also recognize the importance of readers' being able to see themselves in the characters, situations, and language of the stories they read. El día de los niños/El día de los libros is a collaborative effort to reinforce a commitment to linking children to languages, reading, books, and cultures. It is a very flexible and broad-based program that can be tailored in a multitude of ways to implement local programs that encourage bilingualism, sharing of cultures, and enjoyment of the beauty of literature in all of the world's languages. Many libraries start out small, with one short program that recognizes the major language other than English in the community. These programs and celebrations quickly grow to longer, richer programs that attract larger audiences and expand to include other languages and spread throughout the year. Although a lot of attention is paid to Spanish-language programming, El día de los niños/El día de los libros recognizes that all languages are beautiful and should be celebrated. Although the calendar marks Día as being celebrated on April 30, many communities select a different date. The celebration is meant to be a community event and can be tailored to fit local needs and calendars.

History

The roots of the Día celebration can be found in other literary celebrations and literacy programs, including Children's Book Week and National Library Week, as well as in library-based summer-reading programs and programs like the American

Library Association's Every Child Ready to Read project. Typically, these and other literacy programs seek to focus attention on the joy of reading, sharing books, and encouraging literacy. They also serve to celebrate family literacy and to encourage parents and their children to read, often while teaching caregivers about the value of books, library resources, and libraries.

In March 1996, while being interviewed in Tucson, Arizona, author and poet Pat Mora learned about a holiday celebrated in Mexico and in other Latin American countries that celebrates children. She began to think about why there was no similar celebration in the United States. Although there is some debate as to whether the United States has a day to celebrate children, there is certainly nothing similar to Mother's Day or Father's Day. Some churches recognize a Children's Day that dates back to the mid-nineteenth century, but Mora realized that the United States had nothing like the Children's Day that is celebrated in many other countries. That day has its roots in International Children's Day, first celebrated in Turkey in 1920. In subsequent years, following the first World Conference for the Well-Being of Children, held in Geneva in 1925, that celebration has evolved into a series of celebrations held in different countries throughout the world on various dates. These more generalized celebrations usually focus on issues that are broadly related to child welfare. Pat Mora thought about this holiday, and the lack of a similar celebration in the United States, and decided to expand and enhance the concept of Children's Day to promote the joy of books, especially bilingual books, by adding the link to literacy, an essential issue for the well-being of children.

With assistance from members of REFORMA, the National Association to Promote Library and Information Services to Latinos and the Spanish-Speaking, Mora further developed the concept and began to work on planning the first celebration, held on April 30, 1997. Other organizations, including MANA del Norte, a women's group in Santa Fe, New Mexico, and librarians, including Oralia Garza de Cortés and Veronica Myers, quickly offered their support for the celebration. Later, REFORMA voted to endorse the celebration of family literacy and was an early leader in promoting the initiative throughout the United States and Puerto Rico. On April 30, 1997, the first El día de los niños/El día de los libros celebrations were held in Santa Fe, New Mexico; Tucson, Arizona; and El Paso and Austin, Texas.

Following the first celebrations in 1997, the Texas State Library produced a booklet to help librarians plan local programs to celebrate El día de los niños/El día de los libros. That publication was shared with libraries throughout the country and is still available on the Texas State Library's website (http://tsl.state.tx.us/ld/projects/ninos/). In 1998, the W. K. Kellogg Foundation awarded a grant to allow the National Association of Bilingual Education (NABE) to develop a plan for a national campaign to disseminate information on El día de los niños/El día de los libros. By 1999, schools and libraries across the country had begun holding their own celebrations. Pat Mora and her family established the Estela and Raúl Mora Award in honor of their parents to promote El día de los niños/El día de los libros. Also in 1999, young Latinos who were present at a national summit in San Antonio,

Texas, formally and publically requested a day to celebrate children. The National Latino Children's Institute added its name to the list of organizations promoting programs that honor children. Although the institute's emphasis is on broader issues, its interests include reading and education.

In 2000, the first Mora Award was presented to Austin Public Library, in Texas. The American Library Association formalized its support for El día de los niños/ El día de los libros in 2001, when the Association for Library Service to Children (ALSC) applied for and received a W. K. Kellogg Foundation grant to promote El día de los niños/El día de los libros. As a result, ALSC produced a tip sheet for librarians who were launching their own events and a brochure that librarians could distribute to parents. The W. K. Kellogg Foundation awarded a second grant to ALSC in 2002 to produce and distribute another brochure for parents. The W. K. Kellogg Foundation continued its support in 2002 by awarding funds for El Pueblo, a North Carolina advocacy group for Latinos, to initiate a statewide celebration in North Carolina.

In 2003, the W. K. Kellogg Foundation funding enabled the University of Arizona's School of Information Resources to host meetings of a national Día advisory committee and to produce public relations materials in support of the celebration. Also in 2003, the Texas Library Association received funds from the W. K. Kellogg Foundation for a statewide program to promote El día de los niños/ El día de los libros in school and public libraries. This culminated in a tool kit for librarians to use in developing their programs and in small grants to help boost the number of new programs in the state. In 2004, the Kellogg Foundation awarded a third grant to ALSC to continue the work of the University of Arizona.

By 2005, El día de los niños/El día de los libros had become a tradition and had found a permanent home with ALSC. In 2006, Kellogg awarded an unprecedented fourth grant to ALSC to strengthen national awareness and community participation in Día. As the home for Día, ALSC and its members and staff share resources, many of which I mention elsewhere in this book, that support local programs. Moreover, ALSC provides a database of local programs (www.ala.org/ala/mgrps/divs/alsc/ initiatives/diadelosninos/diacelebrations/diacelebrations.cfm) for librarians to see what their peers are doing and to discover new ways to enhance local programs.

In 2007, Target became the first official national sponsor of Día. Through the company's support, libraries received complimentary bilingual brochures about Día. Funding also provided minigrants to help establish or enhance local programs at eight libraries: El Paso (Texas) Public Library, Hennepin County (Minnesota) Library, Public Library of Charlotte-Mecklenburg County (North Carolina), Queens (New York) Public Library, Riverside County (California) Library System, Broward County (Florida) Library System, Providence (Rhode Island) Public Library, and Phoenix (Arizona) Public Library. These libraries continue to provide exemplary programs related to bilingual literacy and El día de los niños/El día de los libros.

In 2008, Dora the Explorer, the children's television character who shares her adventures in learning on public television, was featured on the Día poster, bookmarks, and brochures, bringing Día into the mainstream of popular culture.

Other national sponsors have included the National Council of Teachers of English; Reading Rockets; and publishers like HarperCollins, Random House, Children's Book Press, and Cinco Puntos Press. Support from these sponsors has included distribution of posters and other promotional materials, discounts for libraries purchasing bilingual resources, and the development of guides to assist in program development. Many of these publishers are also in the forefront of publishing work by Hispanic authors and illustrators and translating English-language books into Spanish.

In 2010, the Dollar General Literacy Foundation awarded ALSC a grant to significantly expand Día to include and celebrate a wide variety of cultures. Fifteen minigrants were awarded to the following:

- Bloomington (Illinois) Public Library
- Brevard County Library System, Cocoa, Florida
- Forest Hill (Texas) Public Library
- Fremont Public Library District, Mundelein, Illinois
- Hall County Library System, Gainesville, Georgia
- Jefferson Parish Library, Metairie, Louisiana
- Longmont (Colorado) Public Library
- Nacogdoches (Texas) Public Library
- Paramus (New Jersey) Public Library
- Paul E. Griffin Library, Camden, Mississippi
- Poughkeepsie (New York) Public Library District
- Rachel Kohl Community Library, Glen Mills, Pennsylvania
- Richland County Public Library, Columbia, South Carolina
- Sachem Public Library, Holbrook, New York
- Saginaw Chippewa Indian Tribal Library, Mount Pleasant, Michigan

The year 2011 marks the fifteenth anniversary of a celebration that continues to grow and reach more children and families. Although it is not possible to know with any certainty how many libraries and schools participate in Día celebrations, in the 2010 survey of ALSC and REFORMA members and libraries, called "Serving Multicultural Populations," 34 percent of respondents indicated that their library hosted Día programs. About one-third of respondents stated that they were familiar with the celebration but were not yet sponsoring any Día programming. For the remaining librarians, El día de los niños/El día de los libros is a new and exciting idea to be explored.

Mission

Día's mission is to link all children to books, languages, and cultures through a vision of family literacy. It involves a daily commitment to family literacy that culminates in an annual celebration. That celebration on or near April 30 frequently reflects a year's worth of activities to support and promote the diversity of communities and multicultural reading for children and families.

What sets Día apart from other literacy celebrations is the emphasis on this mission and Pat Mora's vision for a celebration that transcends all cultures and ethnicities. It is the desire of librarians and Día supporters to promote books that reflect our national plurality and the many cultures of our communities.

As the founder of Día, Pat Mora strongly advocates that the activities in libraries, schools, and communities focus on sharing bookjoy, a word she coined. Although working for bookjoy every day may seem ambitious, the work done through Día can have the positive effect of building a community of readers and a culture of literacy that truly reflects all cultures. Several people, including Sara Howrey, formerly of Kenton County (Kentucky) Library, recognize that Día is "not about food, dancing, and music. Día is about literacy in all home languages."[1] According to Freda Mosquera, Broward County (Florida) Library celebrates El día de los niños/El día de los libros "to bring home the message that we value our communities' children and that we want their futures to be grounded in education and made possible by a firm foundation in early literacy experiences."[2] El día de los niños/El día de los libros activities and celebrations can and should be more than simply multicultural programming or celebrations of diversity. The mission of Día reflects the joy that comes from being *able* to read in whatever language is spoken at home or with family, from being literate, from loving language, and from sharing the love of books and reading.

Goals

From the beginning, Pat Mora, REFORMA, and other founding groups have had the same goals for El día de los niños/El día de los libros. These goals include a "daily commitment" to

- honor children and childhood
- promote literacy, the importance of linking *all* children to books, languages, and cultures
- honor home languages and cultures, thus promoting bilingual and multilingual literacy in this multicultural nation, and global understanding through reading
- involve parents as valued members of the literacy team
- promote library collection development that reflects our plurality

Summing up these goals, Día is primarily a framework for connecting children, literature, literacy, and libraries both in the library and out in the community. This can be accomplished through a celebration of heritage and first-language literature. The second overriding goal for Día is outreach, a way to bring the community to the library and the library to the community.

Benefits of Día Programming

There are currently more than three hundred languages spoken in the United States, according to Census data. According to SIL International, a faith-based nonprofit organization that serves language communities worldwide, there are almost seven thousand languages around the world. Although English is one of the major languages spoken around the world, it is clearly not the only language that is important to children and families.

El día de los niños/El día de los libros activities and the emphasis placed on bilingual and multilingual programming supports bilingual literacy and language development. Why is bilingual literacy and language learning important? "The world faces a future of people speaking more than one language, with English no longer seen as likely to become dominant," according to language researcher David Graddol. According to Yale linguist Stephen Anderson, speaking in the same article, multilingualism is "more or less the natural state. In most of the world multilingualism is the normal condition of people."[3] Being familiar with more than one language and encouraging multilingualism is, therefore, increasingly important to U.S. society. These experts also emphasize that, while it is important for those who live in the United States to learn English, doing so should not mean abandoning one's native language. It is clearly important to be literate in one's first language, but it also is important to recognize that literacy occurs in every language, not just in English.

We all develop a major part of our self-image from seeing ourselves in pictures and hearing language that is familiar to us. Reading and sharing books that include positive images of one's culture and that include words that are heard at home or

How Día Benefits Children and Families

Children who are read to regularly become better readers and achieve more in their education. Día programs support families and encourage parents to read to their children in the language they are most comfortable speaking.

Día programs and activities recognize the value of learning in a family's home language. This strengthens the role of parents and caregivers in their child's education.

Children and their families recognize the library as a welcoming environment.

How Día Benefits Libraries and Communities

The community sees the library as a friendly place that offers activities and services that are relevant to all children and families.

The library is recognized as a family-oriented community location that welcomes everyone.

Libraries and library services become connected to other organizations that serve families and children.

Librarians build relationships with members of our community, enabling the library to better serve them and building support for library services.

from one's relatives support a positive sense of self-worth for children from that culture. Those same books help other children explore differences and similarities among cultures.

Most Americans have roots in non-English-speaking countries and cultures, even if we no longer speak the languages spoken there. A person who is literate in one language may more easily become fluent in another language. Being exposed to languages other than English is helpful for making friends in the community and abroad. Nothing ingratiates an American traveler more than trying to speak at least a few words in the language of the country being visited. Many children become interested in studying abroad after being exposed to other cultures and languages. We begin to see how languages are interrelated and how words affect understanding and commonalities, as well as differences.

In many ways, the actual programs, events, activities, and books used for El día de los niños/El día de los libros programs are not any different from what a library is already offering at other times. What sets Día apart is the emphasis it places on recognizing cultural heritage and the ways that participants work throughout the year to build a culture of literacy in the community.

Libraries are part of the education community and, as such, can be intimidating places to nonusers, new immigrants, and people who lack formal education. People often feel that libraries are not there for them, and in some other countries, libraries may in fact be primarily places for members of the formally educated, elite, or financially secure population. Libraries have an obligation to welcome all members of the community, and for some populations this takes more effort. Libraries can be, and should be, the lead agency in developing a Día program and in bringing together partners to create a culture of literacy in the community that embraces people from all ethnicities who are reading in any language spoken in local homes. A major benefit derived from Día programming can be the sense of community, especially a community of literacy, that comes from embracing the richness of other languages.

Día's Founders

Growing out of the World Conference for the Well-Being of Children held in Geneva, Switzerland, in 1925, International Children's Day is celebrated throughout the world. Many countries selected June 1 for their celebration, but Mexico and many Latin American countries settled on April 30 for what they call Día del Niño. This celebration of children never caught on as an official celebration in the United States, which really had no day set aside to celebrate children, as is done for other family members through Mother's Day, Grandparent's Day, or Father's Day. Even though International Children's Day is celebrated in Mexico, it may be unknown to many Mexican American families, especially those who wanted to assimilate into American culture. Other countries, from Australia to Vietnam, also set aside a day to celebrate childhood and focus on improving the lives of children. Although most of these celebrations target one day and focus broadly on the welfare of children, it is the goal of El día de los niños/El día de los libros to make *every day* a day that supports and celebrates children reading.

In 1996, author and poet Pat Mora originated the idea of combining a celebration of children with a celebration of bilingual literacy. During an interview at the University of Arizona in Tucson, someone mentioned to Mora the Mexican holiday Día del Niño. Although Mora grew up in a Spanish-speaking family with roots in Mexico, she was not familiar with the holiday. Mora quickly recognized that in the United States this celebration could focus attention on literacy, an issue that is the cornerstone of the well-being of children in many other areas of life. In part because April 30 has strong ties to International Children's Day in Latino countries and in part because it is the last day of National Poetry Month—and Pat Mora is, among other things, a poet—she settled on this date for the celebration of El día de los niños/El día de los libros. Mora is quick to emphasize, however, that each community should pick a day that works for it. In fact, many libraries hold their culminating celebration on the weekend nearest April 30, and school libraries often select a date following mandated testing and other distracting obligations.

Pat Mora was born in El Paso, Texas, and spent much of her early life along the border between the United States and Mexico. She began her career as a teacher both in the public schools and at the university level. Considered one of the most distinguished Hispanic writers working in the United States, Mora has published her poetry since 1984, and her work is represented in many anthologies.[4] During her successful writing career, Mora began writing for children and young adults. One of her earliest children's books, *Tomás and the Library Lady,* may have helped set the stage for El día de los niños/El día de los libros, as it focuses on the life of a Mexican American boy who discovers the joy of books and literacy through his local public library. It is also fitting that Mora's works of literature reach as broad an audience as El día de los niños/El día de los libros does. She has written books for adults, teenagers, and children of all ages.

Día's founding partner was REFORMA, the National Association to Promote Library and Information Services to Latinos and the Spanish-Speaking. An affiliate of the American Library Association, REFORMA continues to support Día activities through a variety of avenues, including awarding libraries the Estela and Raúl Mora Award in recognition of outstanding programs. Local chapters of REFORMA are often key sponsors or cosponsors of Día programs and events. Other early supporters included the National Association for Bilingual Education (NABE) and MANA, an organization of Latina women.

Very quickly, a nationwide celebration has grown from a simple idea into one of the most successful and rewarding programs sponsored by libraries of all kinds.

Día's Current Reach

Support for El día de los niños/El día de los libros continues to grow. Various organizations have endorsed Día, and local chapters of these organizations are frequent partners with the library. These early partners include NABE, MANA, the National Latina Organization, the National Latino Children's Institute (NLCI), the Texas State Library, and the W. K. Kellogg Foundation. Many state and local governments have passed resolutions in support of Día. In 2005, the National Council of Teachers of English (NCTE) passed a resolution in support of El día de los niños/El día de los libros and agreed to work to support multilingual family literacy programs.

Camila Alire, 2010 president of the American Library Association, recognized that Día has become a "strong and effective model" of family literacy for the Latino community, and her presidential initiative worked to encourage similar and compatible activities within the Ethnic Affiliates of the American Library Association (ALA).[5] Although her family literacy initiative, ALA Family Literacy Focus, advocates for family literacy in conjunction with ALA's Ethnic Affiliates, it was conceived in the spirit of El día de los niños/El día de los libros, to move family literacy beyond the Latino community. This extension considers the goal of extending family and cultural literacy to all minority communities and to the cultural and linguistic heritage of the majority community.

A survey on serving multicultural populations conducted in 2009 by the Association for Library Service to Children revealed that about one-third of the libraries represented by respondents hosted events or programs for El día de los niños/El día de los libros. Although many librarians recognize that patrons represented a wide range of cultures and ethnic groups, only a few include languages other than Spanish in their programs. There is a need to enhance these programs by adding more Día-related events and programs throughout the year so that every day can be a celebration of bilingual literacy and reading. According to some sources, one in five children younger than the age of five speaks a language other than English at home, and 12 percent of the U.S. population is foreign born.[6] Although many libraries are already providing support for bilingual reading, El día de los niños/El día de los libros has the potential to embrace an even larger community of learners!

Members of ALSC and REFORMA have been leaders in the promotion of Día. As a member of either group, consider what you are doing to support local and regional Día programs. REFORMA's Southeast chapter is working to expand Día celebrations through its Sara Howrey minigrants, named in honor of one of the region's most passionate advocates of bilingual literacy. A 2009 survey of ALSC members found that about one-third of the libraries that hosted Día celebrations submitted information on their activities to the ALSC database. Every librarian, but especially ALSC members, can help other libraries develop and enhance their programs by submitting information to the database. Sharing information about your successes will help other librarians develop new programs or expand on what they are already doing. Judy Rohr, of the Topeka and Shawnee County (Kansas) Public Library, said in her application for the 2009 Mora Award, "Like many public libraries, we've struggled to discover how best to reach out to our Latino and Spanish-speaking residents. The El día de los niños/El día de los libros program is key in connecting Hispanic and Spanish-speaking residents . . . to their library."[7]

Notes

1. Sara Howrey (retired librarian), in conversation with the author, June 2, 2010.
2. Freda Mosquera (librarian, Broward County, FL), in conversation with the author, June 30, 2010.
3. "English Won't Dominate as World Language," MSNBC, February 26, 2004, www.msnbc.msn.com/id/4387421.
4. *Contemporary Authors Online*, s.v. "Pat Mora."
5. Family Literacy Focus Model, www.camilaalire.com/documents/FamilyLiteracyFocusModel.pdf.
6. Anneke Forzani, "The Multicultural Library: How Librarians Are Responding to the Needs of Ethnically Diverse Communities," Language Lizard, www.languagelizard.com/v/vspfiles/newsarticle8.htm.
7. Judy Rohr, application for the 2009 Estela and Raúl Mora Award, Topeka and Shawnee County (Kansas) Public Library.

2
Día Now and in the Future

Bringing Other Cultures into Día

Although a lot of what is included in this book, and in most other resources for El día de los niños/El día de los libros, focuses on programming and activities with the Latino community, the ideas and concepts can be, and should be, expanded for other cultures. Pat Mora's idea for Día goes beyond Spanish bilingualism, and it is her dream that Día activities will encourage and promote bilingual reading in every language. Most celebrations still focus heavily on Hispanic cultures, but many libraries are planning and carrying out programs that celebrate not only the major minority cultures—Latino, African American, Asian American, and Native American—but also European and non-Hispanic North American cultures. The work of 2009–2010 ALA President Camila Alire's Family Literacy Focus initiative enhanced Día-type programming through the American Library Association's Ethnic Affiliates—the Asian/Pacific American Librarians Association, the American Indian Library Association, the Black Caucus of the ALA, the Chinese American Librarians Association, and REFORMA.

Many of the examples and descriptions in this book feature the Hispanic community; however, whenever possible, examples for other cultures are included. Día should support all languages that are spoken in homes in your community. Keep in mind that this can change rapidly in today's global society, so take time occasionally to consider whether you should bring other languages into your Día programming. Also don't forget to consider the deaf community and the role of sign language in deaf culture. The Pima County (Arizona) Library's Woods Memorial Branch hosted the Sign and Play program, where families selected their favorite stories to share. After reading or telling the stories, they learned the signs that go

Poem-flowers in the poetry garden at Farmington (New Mexico) Public Library

along with them. The Austin (Texas) Public Library partnered with the Texas School for the Deaf to offer signed storytimes for deaf and hearing families.

ALA president Camila Alire used El día de los niños/El día de los libros as the foundation for her presidential initiative that "focus[es] on a literacy effort that will provide resources to the five ALA ethnic affiliates to develop family literacy projects and programs that can be replicated by libraries throughout the country."[1] Although the programs developed under Alire's leadership are independent, they support and extend the concepts of El día de los niños/El día de los libros.

The Chinese American Librarians Association's project Dai Dai Xiang Chuan: Bridging Generations, a Bag at a Time offers literacy and cultural activities that emphasize verbal and written language skills and cultural and digital literacy to bring generations together. The "bags" developed by librarians include bilingual (Chinese and English) print and digital materials on varied intergenerational topics and include instructions for family activities.

The Black Caucus of the ALA launched Reading Is Grand! Celebrating Grand Families @ your library, targeted at grandparents raising their grandchildren. The focus of the project is very similar to that of El día de los niños/El día de los libros: to foster a lifelong love of reading. The caucus has developed a tool kit and other resources aimed to help all types of libraries plan and implement this literature-based intergenerational literacy program.

Talk Story: Sharing Culture, Sharing History is a library program designed to serve Asian and Asian American, Native Hawaiian, and other Pacific Islander and Pacific Islander American, American Indian, and Alaska Native families. The goal is to bring basic and cultural literacy together by combining storytime and oral traditions, and participants strengthen literacy skills through culturally appropriate materials.

REFORMA uses Noche de Cuentos (Story Night) programming to promote and preserve the art of storytelling within the Latino communities in the United States. Much in line with the goals and objectives of El día de los niños/El día de los libros, Noche de Cuentos programs honor home languages and cultures to promote literacy and the importance of linking storytelling, language, libraries, and cultures.

Communities like Kentucky's Kenton County have a relatively small Hispanic population. So in addition to the community's Spanish speakers, the library worked to include speakers of other languages in its Día programming. Retired librarian Sara Howrey found that people from other countries may have been working to assimilate in the American cultures and therefore did not automatically mention that they speak a language other than English in their family. Howrey found that, when asked, most people are happy to share their language with children and families and become fabulous volunteers for the program, helping with world language storytimes as well as Día celebrations.

If I Can Read, I Can Do Anything, an initiative spearheaded by Loriene Roy at the University of Texas at Austin to encourage Native American children and community members to read for pleasure, has provided support for El día de los niños/El día de los libros programs on Indian reservations. In 2001, each participating school received two books by Native American authors.

Farmington (New Mexico) Public Library frequently includes Native American poetry readings in its celebration of El día de los niños/El día de los libros, or Ałchíní Baa Hózhóogo Bee E'e'aah Naaltsoos Wólta' Bee E'e'aah, in Navajo. As part of the celebration, and as a tie-in with National Poetry Month, Farmington Public Library hosts creative writing sessions and encourages children to write poetry in their native language, usually Spanish or Navajo. Each child creates a poem-flower for the poetry garden. Many of the original poems are gathered into a book, *Saad ak'e'elchí*, which is published by the Northwest New Mexico Arts Council and made available for sale through the council's website (www.nwnmac.org/saadpoetry .html). The library also used its Día celebration as the kickoff event for the New Mexico Youth and Community Summit.

McCall (Idaho) Public Library expanded its Día programming to be a world cultures week at the library. Elementary school students attended workshops during the week and a community street fair was held on Saturday. Cultures represented include Tanzania, Finland, Ecuador, and the Nez Percé nation, among others. A Fulbright scholar from Bosnia gave a lecture, and Los Cenzontles, a band from California with Mexican roots, performed. The library partnered with the American Association of University Women, which provided books from the Carolrhoda series Everybody Cooks by Norah Dooley. Each book, like *Everybody Serves Soup*, depicts children in multicultural neighborhoods eating rice, soup, bread, and noodles in their own traditional way and includes recipes from several cultures that can be replicated at home or in programs. Other partners included the local folklore society and the arts and humanities council.

Translating El día de los niños/El día de los libros into other languages is always a bit tricky, but the following suggestions were vetted through Pat Mora's blog, *bookjoy* (http://sharebookjoy.blogspot.com). Check the site for additional translations, with more to be added. Ask community members to help if a language spoken in your community is not included here. Use the translations as part of a program in which families create minibooks, like the one that follows, in the language that is important to them:

Portugese: Celebrar dia da criança/do livro
Hindi: Bacche ka din/Kitab ka din
Punjabi: Bacche da din/Kitab da din
German: Ein fest von den Kindern und Lesen
Italian: Una celebrazione di bambini e di lettura

My Language Minibook

Use templates for minibooks, such as those provided by Enchanted Learning (www .enchantedlearning.com/books/mini/) to help children create their own book in their own language. Alternatively, a reproducible minibook is available for a small membership fee. Provide patterns for animals, plants, people, and objects, or cut out photographs from old magazines. Make a page for each illustration and then label the illustration with the appropriate word in Spanish, Italian, French, Korean, or whatever language the child would like.

From Cultural Celebration to Celebration of Literacy: Make Every Day a Día Day

In an ideal world, librarians would have time to promote bilingual literacy and cultural literacy every day. The goal of Pat Mora, Día's founder, is to have small celebrations of language permeate all of the activities that occur in the library so that celebrating language becomes second nature. The April 30 celebration can then be a culmination of a year's worth of activities and programs. If April 30 falls on a day that is not appropriate or convenient for programming, pick another day to celebrate!

It's easier said than done, but consider some ways to incorporate the desired effects of Día into other programs that you are already doing. Keeping the concepts and goals of Día in mind and adding elements of Día to ongoing programs also helps to morph the ideas of El día de los niños/El día de los libros from a cultural celebration to a purer celebration of literacy. We are moving toward meeting the goal of Día—linking all children to books, languages, and cultures—by creating a completely inclusive celebration of literacy.

One easy way to expand the Día concept is to include books in other languages or to highlight other cultures for one or more sessions of an ongoing program like storytime. World-language storytimes and bilingual storytimes are already working to achieve some of Día's goals, but the traditional preschool storytime can become a Día event by featuring books, rhymes, and activities from another culture. Even if many of the children in the group don't speak the focus language, they will easily recognize books that are already familiar to them, like *Kot v shliape*, the Russian version of *The Cat in the Hat* by Dr. Seuss. Invite a Russian speaker to be a guest reader.

Include books from other cultures in storytime, afterschool programs, and class visits to the library. Make a simple statement that recognizes the beauty of the words that are included in the story. Kenton County (Kentucky) Public Library uses a single book in multiple languages and has native speakers read the same book sequentially during the storytime. A book like *Splash!* by Flora McDonnell is short enough so that as many as ten or eleven languages can be included in a single program. Each reader reads the first page in sequence and then the second page and so on. A copy of the book is required for each reader, but if a needed language is not available, provide a copy in English in advance for the reader to translate. Look not only for books that are available in multiple translations but also for books that are large in format with big, clear illustrations. According to Lise Tewes, a librarian with Kenton County Public Library, younger children may not fully understand

A reader participates at a bilingual storytime

that they are hearing different languages; they just recognize that they are hearing new words. Tewes also suggests inviting the readers to wear traditional dress or special clothing to further highlight the different cultures.

For a complete program, you may not be able to include only books that are available in another language. In that case, add some culturally authentic books that may include a few words or phrases in the focus language. You might also ask a native speaker or another person who is fluent in the language to translate a few key words for you to add to the book.

Books to Consider

Children of the Yukon, **by Ted Harrison.** This picture book depicts life for children in the Yukon as they work and play in the Arctic.

An Elephant in the Backyard, **by Richard Sobol.** A photojournalist visits a community in Thailand, where he meets an elephant being raised by a human family.

Faraway Home, **by Jane Kurtz.** As her father prepares to return to Ethiopia, a young girl listens to him talk about his homeland.

Gabriella's Song, **by Candace Fleming.** Venice, Italy, is a city of music, and a young girl hears the beauty in voices, water, the church bell, and more.

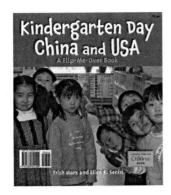

The English cover of *Kindergarten Day China and USA*

Kindergarten Day USA and China/Kindergarten Day China and USA: A Flip-Me-Over Book, **by Trish Marx and Ellen B. Senisi.** After learning about kindergarten in one country, flip the book over to see what is the same and different in the other.

Mama and Papa Have a Store, **by Amelia Lau Carling.** Based on her memories of growing up Chinese in Guatemala, this book allows readers to enjoy the sights and sounds of a city and the interweaving of Spanish, Chinese, and Mayan cultures in a general store.

Mama's Saris, **by Pooja Makhijani.** A little girl helps her mother select a sari for a special event and recalls the significant times when her mother has worn this special outfit. Includes a glossary of Hindi words.

My Farm, **by Alison Lester.** Life on an Australian farm may seem familiar to kids in the United States, but even English has its differences as "drovers" drive a "mob" of cattle.

Seeds of Change: Wangari's Gift to the World, **by Jen Cullerton Johnson.** This picture biography tells the story of Wangari Muta Maathai, the woman who won the 2004 Nobel Peace Prize. Although there are few Kenyan words in the story, it is rich in African culture.

Celebrate Holidays

Use celebrations of cultural holidays to promote bilingual literacy. Although it is typical for libraries to host special programs for commonly celebrated American holidays, don't overlook holidays that are important to other cultures. Ideas for a few are provided here, but *Chase's Calendar of Events* and resources for most countries list holidays and celebration days. Look around your community to see what festivals are being held in the community.

Independence Day: Dieciséis de Septiembre

September 16 marks the day in 1810 that Mexicans began their journey to gain independence from the Spaniards. It is celebrated with patriotic spirit that includes dancing, picnics, and parades. Father Miguel Hidalgo y Castillo rang the church bell in Dolores, Mexico, and beseeched his congregation to oppose Spanish rule. Father Hidalgo made the Virgin of Guadalupe and his famous *grito*—a call to revolution—symbols of Mexican liberation. The day, September 16, has become the kickoff date for Hispanic Heritage Month in the United States but can also be used to show how one culture celebrates an important time in their history.

Today Mexican Independence Day celebrations are infused with music, dancing, and food. Focus on the mission of El día de los niños/El día de los libros by adding a series of programs that feature celebrations of independence in a range of countries in addition to Mexico. Wikipedia has compiled a list of independence days by country (http://en.wikipedia.org/wiki/List_of_national_independence_days).

Books to Consider

Fiesta Babies, **by Carmen Tafolla.** Babies love fiestas, but they also enjoy siestas in this colorful rhyming story.

The Lady of Guadalupe, **by Tomie dePaola.** In 1531, Our Lady of Guadalupe, an apparition of the Virgin Mary, appeared to a poor indigenous farmer in Mexico, and this picture book explores her story.

Mexican Independence Day and Cinco de Mayo, **by Dianne M. MacMillan.** Part of the Best Holiday series, this book explores the history and culture of two important Mexican celebrations.

Stories of Mexico's Independence Days, and Other Bilingual Children's Fables, **edited by Eliseo "Cheo" Torres and Timothy L. Sawyer Jr.** This book includes six bilingual stories with regional and cultural emphases, including two about Mexico's fight for independence from France and Spain. The book includes suggested activities.

Craft: Make a Guitar[2]

Materials: poster board; scissors; pencils; markers; guitar pattern; hole puncher; yarn (to thread through holes to "string" guitar); glitter, sequins, etc., to decorate guitar; glue

A decorated and strung guitar

Guitar pattern for the make-a-guitar craft

Directions: In advance, blow up the guitar pattern on a photocopier to fit a piece of 8½-by-11-inch paper. Older children can trace the pattern onto poster board, or an adult can do this for younger children. Cut out the guitar shape, and cut out the hole in the body. Use the markers to color the guitar. Punch holes for the yarn and then "string" the guitar. Use the glitter and sequins to decorate the guitar.

Song: "De Colores"

The song "De Colores" is often sung as an expression of joy and a celebration of freedom. There are many stanzas, and many artists have recorded the song. Sing as many verses as desired, but this is the standard first verse:

> **De Colores** (traditional)
> De colores,
> De colores se visten los campos en la primavera
> De colores,
> De colores son los pajaritos que vienen de afuera
> De colores,
> De colores es el arco iris que vemos lucir
> Y por eso los grandes amores
> De muchos colores me gustan a mí

Use the lyrics and music from *Songs for Teaching* (www.songsforteaching.com/spanishsongs.htm), to teach this and other songs to the children.

Celebrate Spring: Holi

Holi is celebrated in India to recognize the spring harvest season and to celebrate the end of winter and its mischievous spirits. It is also celebrated in other countries with large Indian populations, and the colorfulness of the holiday makes it a popular choice for sharing with children. The exact date varies by year, and according to the Hindu calendar, Holi takes place during the full moon in late February or early March. Although rooted in Hindu theology, the celebration is not a religious one.

Holi is often celebrated by throwing colored powders and water at one another, a messy endeavor that leaves white clothing covered with bright colors! Because this can be too messy for a library celebration, find other ways to host a carnival of colors. For example, give each child a roll of confetti streamers to throw at one another. Long rolls of thin paper are a lot easier to clean up! Use tissue paper to create brightly colored paper flowers, or use colored ribbons and scarves for a color dance while playing Indian music or singing "Celebrating Holi" by Nancy Stewart. Incorporate colors into a craft such as finger painting or creating paper rainbows.

Extend the celebration of spring to other cultures by considering programs related to the Japanese cherry blossom festival, May Day, or Russia's celebration of Maslenitsa (Pancake Week) when the gloom of winter is pushed out to allow the brightness of spring to enter.

Books to Consider

Children Just Like Me, by **Barnabas Kindersley.** This book explores celebrations all over the world, including Holi.

Here Comes Holi: The Festival of Colors, by **Meenal Pandya.** A mother tells her child the ancient tale of this Hindu holiday.

Holi (Rookie Read-About Holidays), by **Uma Krishnaswami.** Brightly colored photographs help to explain the roots of the colorful Holi celebration and the cultural significance it holds for Indian people.

My Hindu Year (A Year of Religious Festivals), by **Cath Senker.** Moving chronologically through the year, this book looks at the major holidays that Indian families celebrate and the customs that go with each.

Song: "Celebrating Holi," by Nancy Stewart

Lyrics and music are available at Stewart's website (http://nancymusic.com/SOM/2008/celebrating-holi.htm).[3]

Chorus
Children in India, celebrating Holi
Celebrating Holi, and the coming of spring
Families in India gather with their neighbors
Celebrating Holi and the coming of spring

Verses
Dancing and singing, and sweets made for eating
Laughing and welcoming the coming of spring
(Repeat chorus)

Painted in the colors, the colors of the rainbow
Dancing in the colors, the colors of spring.
(Repeat chorus)

Food: Mango Lassi

Lassi is a popular Indian drink served very cold. To make, place four cups of plain yogurt in a blender. Add four cups of canned mango pulp (available in many stores or online), two cups of water, and two tablespoons of sugar. Blend well. Put crushed ice in a tall glass, and fill with the lassi. Serve. For a colorful display, make different flavors of lassi by substituting fresh or frozen strawberries, blueberries, or other fruit for the mango.

Websites

BBC | *www.bbc.co.uk/cbeebies/tikkabilla/stories/rupeetree/*
The British Broadcasting Corporation's storytime website includes a reading of "The Rupee Tree," a tale from India.

Holi Festival | *www.holifestival.org*
This site explains the origins, rituals, and significance of Holi and provides a calendar for the main date of Holi. The site also includes retellings of legends related to Holi and other information about the celebration.

Mango Languages | *www.mangolanguages.com*
This learning tool found in many libraries provides pronunciation guides and audio clips of many languages, including Hindi. The website also offers sample language lessons. Holi is also known as Phagwah (Bhojpuri), Doljatra, and Boshonto Utshob (Bengali). India has at least eighteen official languages with many more regional dialects.

It's a New Year: Sol-Nal

As in many other Asian countries, Korea celebrates the New Year on the first day of the first month of the new lunar year. In addition to welcoming a new calendar, the holiday Sol-nal also serves to renew one's place in the world by honoring ancestors and reestablishing family ties. Begin your program by talking about calendars and the practices of wiping the slate clean to start a new year. Read a book like *New Clothes for New Year's Day*, by Hyun-Joo Bae, which follows a young Korean girl as she dresses and prepares for the holiday.

Many Korean families begin the morning on Sol-nal by donning formal clothing (*hanbok*) and performing rituals to honor their ancestors. Food and drink vary by region but are sometimes laid out according to color. Incense may be burned during the day. After eating and honoring the ancestors and living relatives, the day may be dedicated to play, with kite flying, stick games, and dancing popular choices among children.

For a Día program that celebrates Korean literature and language, invite members of the community to show off their *hanbok*, fans, and other items. If the weather permits, have a kite-flying demonstration or ask a kite club to show various kites and explain how they are made and flown. Serve rice cakes, or ask a restaurant to provide Korean treats.

Books to Consider

***Bee-Bim Bop!* by Linda Sue Park.** Bee-bim bop (or *bibimbap*) is a popular Korean dish that can be made as many ways as there are cooks. This picture book introduces readers to the culinary process as a little girl shops and chops and cooks with her mother.

Bibim Bap for Dinner, **by Laura E. Williams.** Through photographs, readers follow step-by-step directions as a boy and his mother make dinner.

Korean Children's Favorite Stories, **by Kim So-Un.** With new illustrations, this collection of thirteen stories offers many of the most familiar and famous stories from Korea.

The Trip Back Home, **by Janet S. Wong.** This book is a gentle celebration of family bonds that recalls a trip that a young girl makes to visit relatives in rural Korea.

Poetry: "Korean New Year," by Janet S. Wong

When Halmoni, my grandmother, was young
all the girls in her small village
spent the night before the new year cooking
and cooking things up: a slice of gossip
mixed into mandoo dumplings,
wishes simmering in lucky duk gook soup.
They covered their mouths each time they laughed.
By midnight their faces were white with rice flour.

Come dawn: a new dress for everyone, no matter how poor.
Then out to swarm the streets, silk joo muh nee pouches
bouncing as they ran. Door to door they went, knocking.
When the old people came to answer, the children shouted
Happy New Year: *Sae Hae Book Mani Bah Doo Say OH!*
Then they bowed down low, paying their respects.

And for their respect they were paid:
an old man might slip a roll of crisp bills inside the pouch.
An old woman would make you take some sweet bean cake.

Oh, say OH: *Happy New Year!*[4]

Craft: Yut Nori

Yut nori is a traditional Korean stick game that is played on Sol-nal. It is similar in some ways to Parcheesi. Provide materials for the children to play this game, or let older children create their own game board.

Materials: tagboard; craft sticks; sticker dots; self-adhesive stars; markers or colored pens and pencils; game pieces

Directions: Each child will need four craft sticks, twenty-seven sticker dots, one star, and at least two game pieces. In advance, cut the tagboard into 12-by-12-inch squares. The children designate one corner as the starting place by placing a large star sticker on the tagboard. Place the sticker dots along the edge of the board, starting to the right of the star. Seven dots will go along each edge except for the last one. Use markers and pens to decorate the four craft sticks on one side only. The children can also decorate the inside area of the game board, if desired. There are other ways to arrange the game board to make the game more complicated. Look at Medieval Korea (http://medieval-baltic.us/koryut.html) and other websites for additional gameboard layouts.

Two or more players play the game. To play, start with all of the game pieces on the star. Each player takes a turn tossing the four sticks onto the table. The player moves his or her game piece according to the number of sticks that land decorated side up. For example, if all four sticks land with the decorated side facing up, the player moves four dots; if one stick lands decorated side up, the player moves only one space. If a player lands on a dot where another player's piece is, that player must move his or her piece back to the starting point. The first player to make it all the way around the board wins.

Expand this program to include information about how the new year is celebrated in other cultures. Keeping in mind that not all celebrations reflect a year that starts on January 1, the theme of the new year could be the focal point for Día programs throughout the calendar. In many cultures, the new year symbolizes a time of renewal, recommitment, and reconnection. Look for books that represent the cultures and include some of the language, if possible, while focusing on the start of a new year.

Ethiopia celebrates the new year on September 11 because the country follows the Orthodox Julian calendar. On New Year's Eve, young and old sing together and may burn torches or bonfires of dried twigs and leaves. Following religious services on New Year's Day (Enkutatash), the family enjoys a meal of *injera* (a flat bread) and *wat* (stew). Share a book like *Silly Mammo*, by Gebregeorgis Yohannes, a tale, reminiscent of the Jack stories, which is bilingual in English and Amharic, Ethiopia's primary language. Although there are no stories specifically related to Enkutatash, read a story like *Faraway Home*, by Jane Kurtz, or *The Best Beekeeper of Lalibela: A Tale from Africa*, by Cristina Kessler. Say, "Melkam, adis amet" to Ethiopian patrons. A title like *Foods of Ethiopia*, by Barbara Sheen, can be used to add information about food and its place in the culture.

New Year at the Pier, by April Halprin Wayland, focuses on the Jewish New Year, Rosh Hashanah. At that time, Jews are encouraged to reflect on their mistakes of the past year. Many Jews participate in the ceremony of tashlich ("casting away").

The *yut nori* game board

According to Wayland, "We walk to a body of water, sing psalms, and toss pieces of stale bread into the water. Each piece of bread represents something we regret doing in the past year. It can remind us to make amends. But mostly, it is a way of letting go, of creating a clean slate for the coming year. Or as Jews say, 'L'shanah tovah!' 'For a Good Year!'" Additional ideas for activities to use with tashlich are available at Wayland's website (www.aprilwayland.com/new-yearat-the-pier/tashlich/activities/), along with information about New Year's celebrations in other cultures. Wayland wrote the following poem specifically for tashlich, and it includes some Yiddish words.

Poetry: "Says the Seagull," by April Halprin Wayland

Shalom to slowly sinking sun
I sing in salty seagull tongue.
But who're these people on my pier?
I sail, I swoop and then fly near.
They're singing, marching up the pier
I think they did the same last year.
A father gives his girl some bread
she scans the waves then tosses crumbs.
I dive, I catch, I save instead
and . . . yum!
I like this ritual at the pier.
I think I'll meet them every year.
I screech my thanks, and then I hear
"*L'shanah Tovah!* Good New Year!"

Note: Shalom can mean "hello," "good-bye," and "peace." [5]

Books to Consider

The Bravest Flute: A Story of Courage in the Mayan Tradition, by Ann Grifalconi. A young boy is chosen to carry a heavy drum and play the bamboo flute as part of the Mayan New Year's celebration.

Dance, Sing, Remember: A Celebration of Jewish Holidays, by Leslie Kimmelman. Each two-page spread describes one of the major Jewish holidays, including the Jewish New Year, and offers games, foods, music, and dance ideas for each celebration.

Diwali: A Festival of Lights and Fun, by Manisha Kumar and Monica Kumar. This dual-language book (English and Hindi) offers a simple story about a family and their celebration of the Hindu five-day festival of lights that welcomes in the lunar new year in each October or November. Includes a read-along CD that features additional songs.

Shanté Keys and the New Year's Peas, a book about celebrating New Year's Day

A Gift, **by Yong Chen.** The postman brings a bit of her homeland to a homesick girl who is sharing the Chinese New Year and Chinese culture with her family.

Happy New Year, Everywhere! **by Arlene Erlbach.** From Belgium to Iran, this book explores the ways New Year's is celebrated in twenty countries. Each spread includes the pronunciation of the traditional greeting and explains how calendars differ, along with a recipe and craft.

The Runaway Rice Cake, **by Ying Chang Compestine.** The Chang family has enough rice to make just one rice cake for New Year's, but when Momma takes it out of the steamer the cake runs away! The book includes recipes for *nián-gāo,* the good-luck cake that is served to ensure health and good fortune.

Shanté Keys and the New Year's Peas, **by Gail Piernas-Davenport.** Rhyming text highlights an African American family's celebration of New Year's Day with hoppin' John while a young girl learns how other cultures recognize the holiday.

Ten Mice for Tet! **by Pegi Dietz Shea and Cynthia Weill.** Mice prepare for the Vietnamese Tet celebration, from one mouse planning the party to ten mice watching fireworks. Notes provide pronunciation guidance for Vietnamese words and indicate regional variations.

This Next New Year, **by Janet S. Wong.** In a truly multicultural community, a Chinese Korean boy celebrates with friends who are German French and Hopi Mexican.

Books Highlighted

Bae, Hyun-Joo. *New Clothes for New Year's Day.* La Jolla, CA: Kane/Miller, 2007.

Carling, Amelia Lau. *Mama and Papa Have a Store.* New York: Dial Books for Young Readers, 1998.

Chase's Calendar of Events 2011. New York: McGraw-Hill, 2010.

Chen, Yong. *A Gift.* Honesdale, PA: Boyds Mills Press, 2009.

Compestine, Ying Chang. *The Runaway Rice Cake.* New York: Simon and Schuster Books for Young Readers, 2001.

dePaola, Tomie. *The Lady of Guadalupe.* New York: Holiday House, 1980.

Dooley, Norah. *Everybody Serves Soup.* Minneapolis: Carolrhoda Books, 2000.

Erlbach, Arlene. *Happy New Year, Everywhere!* Brookfield, CT: Millbrook Press, 2000.

Fleming, Candace. *Gabriella's Song.* New York: Atheneum Books for Young Readers, 1997.

Grifalconi, Ann. *The Bravest Flute: A Story of Courage in the Mayan Tradition.* New York: Little, Brown, 1994.

Harrison, Ted. *Children of the Yukon.* [Plattsburgh, NY]: Tundra Books, 1977.

Johnson, Jen Cullerton. *Seeds of Change: Wangari's Gift to the World.* New York: Lee and Low Books, 2010.

Kessler, Cristina. *The Best Beekeeper of Lalibela: A Tale from Africa.* New York: Holiday House, 2006.

Kim So-un. *Korean Children's Favorite Stories.* Boston: Tuttle Pub, 2004.

Kimmelman, Leslie. *Dance, Sing, Remember: A Celebration of Jewish Holidays.* New York: HarperCollins, 1999.

Kindersley, Barnabas. *Children Just Like Me.* New York: Dorling Kindersley, 1995.

Krishnaswami, Uma. *Holi.* Rookie Read-About Holidays. New York: Children's Press, 2003.

Kumar, Manisha, and Monica Kumar. *Diwali, khushiyon ka tyohara/Diwali, a Festival of Lights and Fun.* Creating Curiosity. [San Jose, CA]: MeeraMasi, 2006.

Kurtz, Jane. Illus. by Earl B. Lewis. *Faraway Home.* San Diego: Harcourt, 2000.

Lester, Alison. *My Farm.* Boston: Houghton Mifflin, 1994.

MacMillan, Dianne M. *Mexican Independence Day and Cinco de Mayo.* Springfield, NJ: Enslow Publishers, 1997.

Makhijani, Pooja. *Mama's Saris.* New York: Little, Brown, 2007.

Marx, Trish, and Ellen B. Senisi. *Kindergarten Day USA and China/Kindergarten Day China and USA: A Flip-Me-Over Book.* Watertown, MA: Charlesbridge, 2010.

McDonnell, Flora. *Splash!* Cambridge, MA: Candlewick Press, 1999.

Pandya, Meenal Atul. *Here Comes Holi: The Festival of Colors.* Wellesley, MA: MeeRa Publications, 2003.

Park, Linda Sue. *Bee-Bim Bop!* New York: Clarion Books, 2005.

Piernas-Davenport, Gail. *Shanté Keys and the New Year's Peas.* Morton Grove, IL: Albert Whitman, 2007.

Senker, Cath. *My Hindu Year.* A Year of Religious Festivals. New York: PowerKids Press, 2008.

Seuss, Dr. *The Cat in the Hat.* New York: Random House, 1985.

Seuss, Dr., and Vladimir Gandelsman. *Kot v shliape.* St. Petersburg: Kyrlia-Myrlia, 2008.

Shea, Pegi Deitz, and Cynthia Weill. *Ten Mice for Tet!* San Francisco: Chronicle Books, 2003.

Sheen, Barbara. *Foods of Ethiopia.* Detroit, MI: KidHaven Press, 2008.

Sobol, Richard. *An Elephant in the Backyard.* New York: Dutton Children's Books, 2004.

Tafolla, Carmen. *Fiesta Babies*. Berkeley, CA: Tricycle Press, 2010.

Torres, Eliseo "Cheo," and Timothy L. Sawyer Jr., eds. *Stories of Mexico's Independence Days, and Other Bilingual Children's Fables*. Albuquerque: University of New Mexico Press, 2005.

Wayland, April Halprin. *New Year at the Pier: A Rosh Hashanah Story*. New York: Dial Books for Young Readers, 2009.

Williams, Laura E. *Bibim Bap for Dinner*. New York: Bebop Books, 2006.

Wong, Janet S. *This Next New Year*. New York: Frances Foster Books, 2000.

———. *The Trip Back Home*. San Diego, CA: Harcourt, 2000.

Yazzie, Venaya J., comp. *Saad ak'e'elchí': Navajo*. [Farmington]: Northwest New Mexico Arts Council, 2006.

Yohannes, Gebregeorgis. *Silly Mammo: An Ethiopian Tale*. [Oakland, CA]: African Sun Press, 2002.

Notes

1. Camila Alire, "President's Message—Advocacy: Part II," *American Libraries*, October 23, 2009, http://americanlibrariesmagazine.org/columns/presidents -message/advocacy-part-ii.
2. Based on a project created by Brooke Ballard; used with permission.
3. Used with permission.
4. © 2010 Janet S. Wong. Used by permission of the author, who controls all rights.
5. © 2010 April Halprin Wayland, www.aprilwayland.com. Used by permission of the author, who controls all rights.

3
Cultural Competencies

Culture "implies the integrated patterns of human behavior that includes thoughts, communications, actions, customs, beliefs, values, and institutions of racial, ethnic, religious, or social groups."[1] Our own culture, our ethnicity, socioeconomic condition, and language influence the way we think, behave, and are.

Cultural competency refers to the ability to interact effectively with people from other cultures. These competencies comprise behaviors, attitudes, and beliefs that form a foundation for the policies and practices that define the quality of services provided in libraries and other organizations. There are generally several components to cultural competency:

- awareness of one's own cultural values and viewpoint
- personal attitude toward cultural differences
- knowledge about other cultures and other points of view
- awareness of cross-cultural dynamics
- ability to adapt interactions on the basis of diversity between cultures

Ghada Elturk asks, "Can diversity be implemented in the absence of cultural competency?" Elturk points out that "the first step in cultural competency is in acknowledging the fact that we don't know enough about other cultures. Then we need to agree that different people have different experiences, viewpoints and stories, sometimes contradictory ones."[2] Therefore, to value diversity, one must first accept and respect differences.

The world does not function under a single set of beliefs and values. From an anthropological perspective, different cultures define value systems as basic as family differently. Knowing something about the value systems and practices of the cultures represented in our communities will help us communicate better with patrons and provide a higher quality of services that meet patrons' individual needs. It is imperative, however, that the knowledge about the community come from authentic sources—the people you want to serve.

Being aware of our cultural viewpoint can also help us to understand how our actions might affect people from other cultures. We can use our understanding of cultural differences to adapt activities to fit different cultural norms. It might be said that the United States has never really been a homogeneous country; people immigrated here from all over the world and, of course, Native people were already here when Europeans first arrived in the Americas. The Native people were and still are very diverse. So even though as a nation we have always been pretty diverse, it is also accurate that we are becoming even more diverse every year. This adds to the need for organizations and their staff to be even better at working with people from different cultures. Being able to reach out to people who are different from us in an effective and appropriate manner is important to the success of any library program, including El día de los niños/El día de los libros.

Although some aspects of cultural identity are broad, we must also remember that within any culture there will also be diversity. Not every person from Mexico holds all of the same values and beliefs, any more than every person from Italy enjoys the same foods. Economics, education, geographical location, and gender may heavily influence how cultural practices have evolved and manifest, so librarians must be careful about overgeneralizing cultural practices and mores. Often we are reluctant to offer programming directed to a specific group or groups of people exactly because of that diversity within a culture. However, as Oralia Garza de Cortés, a Latino children's literature consultant, often points out, it is not what you offer so much as how you make the offer that will make the difference. Develop an understanding of the cultures in your community. Try to gain an understanding of those community members' point of view by inviting members of the community into the planning of your programs. One of the most important things to do is start small—invite families to smaller events and activities first so that they can meet the library's staff.

Studies have shown that in many areas of life, but especially in education, members of minority groups may need extra reinforcement and support to be successful. Not every family celebrates cultural events in the same way, and it is possible that as part of their efforts to assimilate into the broader American culture, families shut the door on some of their own cultural celebrations. However, research also indicates that in the United States, members of racial and ethnic minorities rely heavily on libraries for their information needs. That dependency and the trust that ensues can go a long way toward helping librarians promote bilingual reading and literacy.

In her article "Serving Multicultural Populations by Increasing Our Cross-Cultural Awareness in Libraries: Japan and the USA Serving Latin Americans, Brazilians, Latinos and Hispanics," Sandra Rios Balderrama rightly points out that we are all works in progress when it comes to cultural competencies. We may be able to achieve success in only a few areas of competency. As Balderrama concludes, "Even a basic desire by a local librarian to reach out to people that he sees that are new in the community" creates a place that is welcoming to families who are "interested in learning about world cultures and literature through books, the Internet, newspapers, DVDs, and programs."[3]

The American Library Association's Office for Diversity offers assistance to libraries in learning how to foster diversity and to be inclusive in activities and access to services. The office's website (www.ala.org/ala/aboutala/offices/diversity/diversityplanning.cfm) offers resources for incorporating cultural competencies into all areas of library management.

Although not structured specifically for educational and library organizations, the National Center for Cultural Competence, housed at Georgetown University, offers some checklists for assessing cultural competencies that may be helpful to people outside the health and mental health fields, the main audience for its work. For example, the checklist "Promoting Cultural Diversity and Cultural Competency: Self-Assessment Checklist for Personnel Providing Behavioral Health Services and Supports to Children, Youth and Their Families" (www11.georgetown.edu/research/gucchd/nccc/documents/ChecklistBehavioralHealth.pdf) includes many topics relevant to early childhood education in libraries.

To ensure that families who speak languages other than English feel comfortable and welcome in the library and at your programs, consider these tips:

- If possible, have staff members who speak the language assisting with programs. If staff members are not available, try to find volunteers or contract with an on-call translation service like many hospitals and medical facilities do. Keep a list of basic words and phrases available. Health-care providers and emergency services personnel routinely make up these types of lists, and librarians can as well. See an example of a library phrase list in Spanish at the Learning Light (www.thelearninglight.com/LibraryPhraseLists.pdf). Even a simple one-page list of phrases and words with pictures will help.
- Make an effort to learn parents' and children's names and to pronounce them correctly.
- Include images that reflect the diversity of your community in graphics on flyers and handouts, in photographs on the website, and in advertisements.
- Post signs and flyers in the languages spoken in your community.
- Provide staff development on diversity and cultural awareness. Include information about sensitivity to cultural and language differences that staff members should take into consideration when greeting and working with people who speak a language other than English. Demonstrate cultural etiquette and business protocols so that staff are aware of differences. For example, in some cultures, it is impolite to look a person directly in the eyes, whereas in American culture that can be interpreted as not paying attention.

- Ask families what language they would prefer to receive information in. If possible, work to provide information in the preferred language. Take advantage of community volunteers and translating services to ensure that basic library documents (like library card applications) are available in the languages spoken in your community. Rewrite English-language flyers, forms, and handouts for parents in simple language and vocabulary. Also include graphics to help less proficient English speakers understand your meaning.
- Display books and other materials during programs that reflect the diversity of your community.

In addition to having a collection of books that reflect the diverse languages in your community, be sure to have authentic music from the cultures represented in the community. Remember that even though members of different cultures may speak the same language, such as Spanish, the cultural materials from different regions and countries may be quite different. Have props, such as dolls and puppets, that reflect children from different cultures available for play in the children's area and for use during storytimes and other programs.

Training Staff

All of the programs in the world may go unattended or be less than successful if staff members don't understand how to interact with and be respectful of people from other cultures. In training staff and volunteers in cultural competencies, begin by taking one or more of the assessments provided by groups like the National Center for Cultural Competence (www11.georgetown.edu/research/gucchd/nccc/documents/ChecklistBehavioralHealth.pdf). The checklist helps to challenge the status quo and raise issues that may need to be addressed within your organization. Checklists also test our assumptions about our own and other cultures.

Cultural competency begins with self-reflection and an understanding that we are not all culturally identical. It moves on to an understanding, acceptance, and appreciation of cultural issues. In training and professional development of cultural competencies, it is important that staff have opportunities to get to know people from other cultures. Supervisors and directors can encourage staff to participate in community events and get out of the library to meet members of the varied cultural communities the library serves. In her article "Cultural Competence: A Conceptual Framework for Library and Information Science Professionals," Patricia Montiel Overall looks more closely at the need for, and lack of, training in cultural competencies for library professionals and proposes a conceptual framework for developing cultural competence.[4]

Invite staff and community volunteers to share information about their seasonal or holiday customs and practices. This sharing can lead to discussions that help staff understand cultural differences and similarities.

Encourage staff to review customer-service training modules that deal with serving a diverse community. Two examples are module 2 of the Houston Area Library System's online course, Customer Service 123 (www.hals.lib.tx.us/cust123/2diversity.htm), and module 2 of Marketing 123 (www.hals.lib.tx.us/plan123/2intro.htm), both of which look at how to ensure success in working with diverse customers. Training organizations like WebJunction (www.webjunction.org) and LE@D (www.leadonline.info) offer training resources, free or for a small fee, that can be used to help staff achieve cultural competency.

Consider and review documents like the Guidelines for Library Services to Spanish-Speaking Library Users, developed by ALA's Reference and User Services Association (www.ala.org/Template.cfm?Section = specialpop&template = /ContentManagement/ContentDisplay.cfm&ContentID = 152658). Develop a plan to "grade" the library on its strengths and weaknesses in each area. Although aimed at businesses in general, Diversity Central also offers a tool kit for managers (www.diversityhotwire.com/leaders_toolkit/toolkit/) that offers ideas for improving diversity in the workplace. The website also provides diversity quizzes and calendars. Use some of these resources in staff training.

Collection Development

A major part of ensuring that the library and its staff are welcoming to people from other cultures includes creating a high-quality collection of bilingual and culturally authentic children's materials. Although it has become easier for libraries in the United States to build Spanish-language collections, and there are good resources like *Libros esenciales,* by Tim Wadham, and *Recommended Books in Spanish for Children and Young Adults: 2004–2008,* by Isabel Schon, available to guide librarians, it can be more difficult to find high-quality material in other languages. Be persistent! Ask colleagues for help. Consult resources like *Windows on the World: International Books for Elementary and Middle Grade Readers,* by Rosanne Blass, which feature outstanding international books and winners of awards from other countries. The University of Arizona's journal *WOW Review: Reading across Cultures* (http://wowlit.org/on-line-publications/review/) features titles that are culturally authentic by area.

Visit with vendors at national conferences. The American Library Association conferences always include myriad non-U.S. publishers, distributors, and bookstores. If you can't attend the conference, check out the exhibitor guide online. In some cases, as with Spanish books in past years, you may have to sacrifice a bit on quality of bindings or bypass normal selection policies and procedures to have some books in the languages spoken in your community, but do your best. Ask patrons for recommendations, and ask patrons and distributors to suggest stories that are popular in their home country.

A sampling of major sources for purchasing non-English-language books is included in the "Resources" section of this book.

Formats of Books

There are several types of books to consider for your world languages or multilingual collection and programs. These include books purchased in the original language, translations of books published originally in English, and books that include code switching—the embedding of words in another language in a book that is otherwise written predominantly in English.

Translations

Translations of books originally published in English in the United States are somewhat easier to find, and in fact several titles, a few of which are listed here, are available in multiple languages, thus making it easy to share a familiar story in multiple languages. These books, however, are not usually culturally authentic, and even the best translator sometimes stumbles on rhymes and poetry, and some concepts or words just don't translate well from English to another language. These books are rarely written by people from the culture portrayed, but they are often stories with universal appeal. Also, not every book translates successfully into another language. Beyond the art of translating words to retain their original meaning, linguistic nuance, and the cadence of the language, some forms of humor or situations lose context and meaning in translation.

Some translated titles are single-language books, and others are bilingual or dual language, combining the English version with a parallel text that has been translated. Books published simultaneously in English and another language frequently have had as much attention paid to the translation as to the editing of the English-language book.

A Sampling of Books in Multiple Translations

Brian Wildsmith's Farm Animals, **by Brian Wildsmith.** Available in ten languages, including Navajo, French, and Tagalog.

Brown Bear, Brown Bear, **by Bill Martin, illustrated by Eric Carle.** Available in more than a dozen languages, including Urdu, Kurdish, and Tamil.

Carry Me: Babies Everywhere, **by Rena D. Grossman.** Available in six languages, including Amharic, Somali, and Vietnamese.

Elmer's Friends, **by David McKee.** Available in multiple languages, including Gujarati and Arabic.

Farmer Duck, **by Martin Waddell.** Available in more than a dozen languages, including Bulgarian, Persian, Malayalam, and Italian.

The Giant Turnip, **by Henriette Barkow.** Available in more than twenty languages, including German, Czech, Russian, and Urdu.

Head, Shoulders, Knees, and Toes, **by Annie Kubler.** Available in nineteen languages, including Irish, Polish, and Farsi.

Row, Row, Row Your Boat, **by Annie Kubler.** Available in more than a dozen languages, including Hmong, Russian, and Chinese.

Too Many Pears! **by Jackie French.** Available in Japanese, Portuguese, and Spanish.

Where's the Puppy? **by Cheryl Christian.** Available in seven languages, including Vietnamese, Russian, and Haitian Creole.

Embedded Text or Code Switching

Code switching is the practice of moving between different languages in different situations. It is the ability to use two or more languages, or dialects of a language, in the same conversation. Books that include code switching integrate, or embed, words from the second language into the story, flawlessly adding a definition of the word in Spanish, Italian, Greek, or some other language. Usually the word is first introduced in the primary language, but it may later be repeated without translation. These books may also include a glossary with pronunciation guide to help nonspeakers of the language be better readers. Many speakers of multiple languages code switch in their everyday conversations, moving seamlessly between two or more languages.

A Sampling of Picture Books

Before You Were Here, Mi Amor, **by Samantha R. Vamos.** Speaking to her child in both English and Spanish, a mother explains the preparations and excitement leading up to the child's birth.

Crêpes by Suzette, **by Monica Wellington.** Mixed-media collage illustrates this story about a girl in Paris.

Dumpling Soup, **by Jama Kim Rattigan.** Feeling like she is from a "chop suey" family, a girl from a Korean-Chinese-Japanese-Hawaiian-Anglo family prepares dumplings for New Year's. Includes a glossary.

Finders Keepers? **by Robert A. Arnett.** During a trip in India, a man loses his wallet, but a young boy who wants no reward returns it.

Jalapeño Bagels, **by Natasha Wing.** A boy picks out an assortment of baked goods from his family's bakery to bring to school for International Day. Includes Spanish and Yiddish vocabulary.

Margaret and Margarita/Margarita y Margaret, **by Lynn Reiser.** In the park, two children hold identical conversations about having no one to play with until they discover that speaking different languages is no barrier to having fun.

Mrs. Katz and Tush, **by Patricia Polacco.** An elderly Jewish woman becomes friends with her young African American neighbor.

Rubia and the Three Osos, **by Susan Middleton Elya.** This story offers *un buen* twist on an old tale about a girl and three bears.

Silent Music, **by James Rumford.** Living in Baghdad, an Iraqi boy describes many of his favorite things, including his calligraphy pen.

Skippyjon Jones, **by Judy Schachner.** A hyperactive Siamese kitten has a very active imagination. Sent to his room, Skippyjon imagines he is a Chihuahua who has adventures with his amigos.

Time to Pray, **by Maha Addasi.** The muezzin calling the faithful to prayer awakens a Muslim child. Her grandmother makes her prayer clothes and buys her a prayer rug in this picture book that features text in English and Arabic.

What Did Abuela Say? **by Karen Valentin.** Allie loves the food she eats when she visits her *abuelo* and *abuela,* but she doesn't understand the stories they tell her in Spanish.

The Woman in the Moon, **by Jama Kim Rattigan.** This Hawaiian folktale explains the diverse designs of tapa cloth and includes many Hawaiian words.

A Sampling of Read-Aloud Books and Independent Reading

The Avion My Uncle Flew, **by Cyrus Fisher.** This Newbery -honor book is set in post–World War II France and mixes French and English words as a young American boy gets to know his French grandmother.

Before We Were Free, **by Julia Alvarez.** Twelve-year-old Anita de la Torre reflects on what life was like in a dictatorship and her father and uncles' involvement in a plot to kill El Jefe, the dictator of the Dominican Republic.

The Birchbark House, **by Louise Erdrich.** The daily life of an Ojibwa girl is described in this historical tale that includes many Ojibwa words.

Confetti Girl, **by Diana López.** Lina has a sock obsession and a major crush on a sixth-grade classmate, but in a house filled with books, she struggles with major questions, including whether her father loves his books more than he loves her.

Friends of the Heart/Amici del cuore, **by Kate Banks.** A young girl remembers summers spent in Italy with a friend and how their world was changed by his death.

Zapato Power: Freddie Ramos Takes Off, **by Jacqueline Jules.** Freddie's shoes, his *zapatos,* give him super speed, but is he ready to be a hero?

Concept-Bilingual Books

Dawn Jeffers, in her article, "Bilingual Books for ESL Students . . . and Beyond," identifies another type of book, concept-bilingual books.[5] These books take a single concept, such as counting, and focus strictly on it. Jeffers notes that concept-bilingual books offer a rewarding way for children to learn something simple in more than one language, and the books frequently use humor to help children retain the concepts and language. Other concept-bilingual books might look at colors or animals—simple concepts that may already be familiar to a child in one language and so are more easily translated into a second or third language. It is also rather simple to create your own concept-bilingual books if the language you need is not available. Ask a parent or other person who speaks the language to help translate the words or translate simple words using a dictionary. Concept-bilingual books are also great models for allowing children to create their own mini-Pictionary game.

A Sampling of Concept-Bilingual Books

Come Out and Play: Count around the World in Five Languages, **by Diane Law.** The numerals in this multilingual book are shown with color-coded words in English, Spanish, German, French, and Chinese. The illustrations provide the story by encouraging more counting and close examination.

How Many Donkeys? An Arabic Counting Tale, **by Margaret Read MacDonald and Nadia Jameel Taibah.** In this Saudi Arabian folktale, a number of donkeys are loaded with dates to take to the market. But how many donkeys are there? By the end of the story, readers can count in Arabic.

Jambo Means Hello: Swahili Alphabet Book, **by Muriel Feelings.** This alphabet book includes pronunciations of the words used to illustrate each letter along with the cultural concepts related to the customs described.

El pez arco iris opuestos/Rainbow Fish Opposites, **by Marcus Pfister.** Rainbow Fish may be a familiar sea creature, and in this book, he discovers the concept of opposites in Spanish and English.

Wordless Books

Although it may sound oxymoronic, wordless books are very effective for multilingual programs. This category can also include picture books with very limited words, as they are easily translatable. A book like *Come Out and Play: Count around the World in Five Languages*, by Diane Law, has very limited text—only the words for the numerals—and therefore encourages language development through the retelling by different speakers. Wordless picture books can also be used to show aspects of a different culture, which invites native speakers of the languages to add details about the concepts seen in the book.

A Sampling of Wordless Books

Anno's Journey, **by Mitsumasa Anno.** Take a tour of Europe, seeing the architecture, landscapes, children playing, and more along the way.

Last Night, **by Hyewon Yum.** A young Korean girl is sent to bed without supper and, comforted by her bear, begins an imaginary journey into the forest.

Ocean Whisper/Susurro del océano, **by Dennis Rockhill.** A fishbowl and a poster transform a boy's room into an ocean of wonder. Although the story is wordless, the author includes a full-length poem and reading tips in English and Spanish.

Pancakes for Breakfast, **by Tomie dePaola.** Although this book doesn't identify a specific culture, many of dePaola's books reflect his Italian ancestry. This wordless story follows an old woman as she gets all of the ingredients to make pancakes, a truly multicultural food.

Original-Language Publications

Speakers of languages other than English want to read the same books that their peers are reading, and so translations of the Harry Potter books or *Goodnight Moon* are essential to the collection. But readers also want to read books that originated in their own cultures.

Books written and published in another language can be difficult to obtain in the United States. Even more difficult for most librarians is selecting books in a language they don't read when reviews are not readily available. Specialty distributors, some of which are listed in the "Resources" section of this book, can help. The staff at these companies, while trying to sell books, are very aware of which books are well done and which are ephemeral, and they can be of great help. Exhibitors at national conferences can also provide help, and the American Library Association and the Public Library Association conferences, as well as some state conferences, like those of the California and Texas library associations, have exhibitors who sell books published originally in Mexico, Spain, France, Germany, India, China, and other countries. Larger libraries may send staff to international book fairs, such as those in Frankfurt, Germany, and Guadalajara, Mexico. Check also to see if books are included in a cooperative online catalog, like the Online Computer Library Center's WorldCat (www.worldcat.org), or other databases that may give you some indication as to the popularity and availability of the book.

Another source for books published in other countries might be stores in the local communities. Grocery stores that cater to cultural communities often carry books published in the country of origin. Also, larger cities with major populations of speakers of another language may have bookstores that stock exactly what your community wants. Even if you can't travel to Los Angeles, for example, you can shop at Ketab (www.ketab.com), the largest bookstore selling books in Farsi outside of Iran. Call or e-mail bookstores for assistance; the staff are generally happy to help. A list of some bookstores is provided later in this chapter.

Just as with translations of English-language books that libraries obtain from foreign publishers, books originally published in another country may have issues that librarians need to take into consideration. Often, the bindings are paperback or of poorer quality. The books may be more expensive than similar titles from U.S. publishers. Librarians must weigh these factors against the greater value of having books that speak to the community and reflect the values and preferences of their patrons.

Online Resources and E-Books

Children's Books Online | *www.childrensbooksonline.org*
This project is designed as an online library for all of the world's children. It includes translations of books in many languages, including "dead" languages. Although many of these historical books (published before 1930) will not be familiar to most children, the site includes some fairy tales and folktales, along with a number of Beatrix Potter stories.

Chinese Stories Online | *www.panap.com/Chinese_Stories_Online_s/14.htm*
Part of the Pan Asian Publications website, this page provides a number of stories and books free online in English, English and Chinese, and English and another language.

International Children's Digital Library | *http://en.childrenslibrary.org*
This project includes licensed copies of books from around the world, contributed by authors, illustrators, and publishers, to share the world's literature and languages with children. It also provides a good selection tool for books to add to the collection in physical format.

Magazines

Magazines offer quick reading on current topics and may attract reluctant readers. Although there are not a lot of magazines readily available that are geared to young readers from other cultures, there are a few. Look for additional titles in ethnic bookstores, and ask parents if they subscribe to any at home.

Faces | *www.cobblestonepub.com/magazine/FAC/*
Although this magazine is published in English, it shows young readers how people in other countries, regions, and places live. Teacher's guides, available on the website, also offer ideas for multicultural programming.

Iguana | *www.nicagal.com/iguana/eng/*
Entirely in Spanish, articles feature interviews with Latino personalities, short stories, projects, and crafts.

Kahani | *www.kahani.com*
This is a "literary magazine illuminating the richness and diversity that South Asian cultures bring to North America." It includes stories, art, and activities relevant to the Indian and South Asian communities. It also includes reviews of books with South Asian themes or settings.

Skipping Stones | *www.skippingstones.org*
This multicultural magazine offers a forum for youths from different cultures and countries to share their writing and ideas. Each issue includes poems, stories, and drawings and photos from around the world, along with book reviews and a guide for parents and teachers.

Review Sources

Unfortunately, few review sources are readily available for books in other languages. Standard journals, such as *School Library Journal, Booklist,* and the *Horn Book,* may review many dual-language and bilingual books. Many of these books are also included in databases such as Children's Literature Comprehensive Database, which allows searchers to limit searches by language. Some wholesalers, like Baker and Taylor, provide selection assistance for books in Spanish, but unfortunately not for other languages.

In lieu of reviews, use these basic criteria to select other books:

Literary quality—How well is the book written? In an age of electronic searching, consider the writer. Is the writer well known and respected in the home country?

Artistic quality—How does the book look? Especially for picture books, look for good illustrations, a match between the style of art and the story, and the design of the book.

Potential appeal to the reader—Will the reader enjoy the book? This is subjective, but does the overall design and layout of the book look inviting?

To these standard criteria, try to add the quality of translation. For languages like Spanish that have national and regional dialects, try to determine whether the translation will be acceptable to local readers. Many books attempt to have a neutral dialect to avoid regional issues. Again, it may be possible to learn something about a translator's reputation by searching online. The University of Arizona's journal *WOW Review* also shares the criteria their reviewers use for analyzing cultural authenticity (http://wowlit.org/wp-content/media/cultural-authenticity-criteria.pdf).

Barahona Center | *www2.csusm.edu/csb/*
This academic center at California State University–San Marcos promotes literacy in English and Spanish. One of its projects is a database of recommended books in Spanish or about Latinos.

Criticas | *www.libraryjournal.com/csp/cms/sites/LJ/Reviews/Spanish/*
Following the suspension of *Criticas, School Library Journal* offers bimonthly reviews of children's books in Spanish, available online and in the print journal.

Multicultural Review | *www.mcreview.com*
The books reviewed in this quarterly journal deal with multicultural topics but are not necessarily bilingual.

WOW Review: Reading across Cultures | *http://wowlit.org/on-line-publications/review/*
WOW Review is an electronic journal, published by the University of Arizona, that includes critical reviews of children's and adolescent literature that highlights intercultural understanding and global perspectives. The online database of titles is searchable by region as well as by age and genre.

Language Bookstores

Most bookstores are happy to sell to libraries, although they may not offer the discounts librarians are accustomed to getting from library wholesalers. Only a few stores are listed here, but an Internet search can usually find a store selling books in whatever language is needed. Somewhere in the United States there is a significant-enough population of speakers and readers to support a store for almost any language!

ABC Kinderladen | *www.abckinderladen.com*
This Washington-based bookstore specializes in children's books and music from Germany, including a few bilingual titles.

Alphabet Garten | *www.alphabet-garten.com*
Based in New Jersey, this bookstore offers authentic German books and music, as well as translations for children of all ages.

Del Sol Books | *www.delsolbooks.com*
This company, based in San Diego, California, was started by author Alma Flor Ada. It is now primarily an online bookstore selling Ada's books as well as other bilingual and Spanish-language materials.

French and European Publications | *www.frencheuropean.com*
Although the physical store is no longer open, this New York business still sells French children's books by mail order.

Ketab | *www.ketab.com*
Located in Los Angeles, this company is the largest bookstore outside of Iran selling books in Farsi.

Polish Bookstore and Publishing | *www.polbook.com*
Located in Brooklyn, New York, this bookstore features everything Polish, including a small collection of children's books.

Schoenhof's Foreign Books | *www.schoenhofs.com*
Founded in 1856, this store in Cambridge, Massachusetts, has gathered one of the biggest selections of foreign books in North America. Most for children are available in Spanish, German, French, and Italian.

World Language Resources | *www.worldlanguage.com*
This Los Angeles–based store carries children's books in seventy-six languages, along with games and classroom resources to learn languages.

Books Highlighted

Addasi, Maha. *Time to Pray.* Honesdale, PA: Boyds Mills Press, 2010.

Alvarez, Julia. *Before We Were Free.* New York: Alfred A. Knopf, 2002.

Anno, Mitsumasa. *Anno's Journey.* Cleveland, OH: Collins-World, 1978.

Arnett, Robert A. *Finders Keepers? A True Story.* Columbus, GA: Atman Press, 2003.

Banks, Kate. *Friends of the Heart/Amici del cuore.* New York: Farrar, Straus, and Giroux, 2005.

Barkow, Henriette. *The Giant Turnip.* London: Mantra, 2008.

Blass, Rosanne J. *Windows on the World: International Books for Elementary and Middle Grade Readers.* Santa Barbara, CA: Library Unlimited/ABC-CLIO, 2010.

Christian, Cheryl. *Where's the Puppy?* Peek-a-Boo! New York: Star Bright Books, 1996.

dePaola, Tomie. *Pancakes for Breakfast.* New York: Harcourt Brace Jovanovich, 1978.

Elya, Susan Middleton. *Rubia and the Three Osos.* New York: Disney/Hyperion Books, 2010.

Erdrich, Louise. *The Birchbark House.* New York: Hyperion Books for Children, 1999.

Feelings, Muriel L. *Jambo Means Hello: Swahili Alphabet Book.* New York: Dial Press, 1974.

Fisher, Cyrus. *The Avion My Uncle Flew.* New York: Scholastic, 1993.

French, Jackie. *Too Many Pears!* New York: Star Bright Books, 2003.

Grossman, Rena D. *Carry Me: Babies Everywhere.* [New York]: Star Bright Books, 2009.

Jules, Jacqueline. *Zapato Power: Freddie Ramos Takes Off.* [Park Ridge, IL]: Albert Whitman, 2010.

Kubler, Annie. *Head, Shoulders, Knees, and Toes.* Auburn, ME: Child's Play International, 2001.

———. *Row, Row, Row Your Boat.* Baby Board Books. Swindon, U. K. : Child's Play, 2003.

Law, Diane. *Come Out and Play: Count around the World in Five Languages.* New York: NorthSouth Books, 2006.

López, Diana. *Confetti Girl.* New York: Little, Brown, 2009.

MacDonald, Margaret Read, and Nadia Jameel Taibah. *How Many Donkeys? An Arabic Counting Tale.* Morton Grove, IL: Albert Whitman, 2009.

Martin, Bill. *Brown Bear, Brown Bear, What Do You See?* New York: Henry Holt, 1992.

McKee, David. *Elmer's Friends.* New York: Lothrop, Lee, and Shepard, 1994.

Pfister, Marcus. *El pez arco iris opuestos/Rainbow Fish Opposites.* New York: NorthSouth Books, 2006.

Polacco, Patricia. *Mrs. Katz and Tush.* New York: Bantam Books, 1992.

Rattigan, Jama Kim. *The Woman in the Moon: A Story from Hawaii.* Boston: Little, Brown, 1996.

———. *Dumpling Soup.* Boston: Little, Brown, 1993.

Reiser, Lynn. *Margaret and Margarita/Margarita y Margaret.* New York: Greenwillow Books, 1993.

Rockhill, Dennis. *Ocean Whisper/Susurro del Océano.* [Green Bay, WI]: Raven Tree Press, 2005.

Rumford, James. *Silent Music: A Story of Baghdad.* New York: Roaring Brook Press, 2008.

Schachner, Judy. *Skippyjon Jones.* New York: Dutton Children's Books/Penguin Young Readers Group, 2003.

Schon, Isabel. *Recommended Books in Spanish for Children and Young Adults, 2004–2008.* Lanham, MD: Scarecrow Press, 2009.

Valentin, Karen. *What Did Abuela Say?* East Orange, NJ: Marimba, 2009.

Vamos, Samantha R. *Before You Were Here,* Mi Amor. New York: Viking, 2009.

Waddell, Martin. *Farmer Duck.* Cambridge, MA: Candlewick Press, 1991.

Wadham, Tim. *Libros esenciales: Building, Marketing, and Programming a Core Collection of Spanish Language Children's Materials.* New York: Neal-Schuman Publishers, 2007.

Wellington, Monica. *Crêpes by Suzette.* New York: Dutton Children's Books, 2004.

Wildsmith, Brian. *Brian Wildsmith's Farm Animals.* New York: Star Bright Books, 2001.

Wing, Natasha. *Jalapeño Bagels.* New York: Atheneum Books for Young Readers, 1996.

Yum, Hyewon. *Last Night.* New York: Farrar, Straus, and Giroux, 2008.

Notes

1. Mark A. King, Anthony Sims, and David Osher, "How Is Cultural Competence Integrated in Education?" Center for Effective Collaboration and Practice, http://cecp.air.org/cultural/Q_integrated.htm.
2. Ghada Elturk, "Diversity and Cultural Competency," *Colorado Libraries* 29 (Winter 2003): 5–7.
3. Sandra Rios Balderrama, "Serving Multicultural Populations by Increasing Our Cross-Cultural Awareness in Libraries: Japan and the USA Serving Latin Americans, Brazilians, Latinos and Hispanics," Current Awareness Portal, http://current.ndl.go.jp/node/14412.
4. Patricia Montiel Overall, "Cultural Competence: A Conceptual Framework for Library and Information Science Professionals," *Library Quarterly* 79 (April 2009): 175–204.
5. Dawn Jeffers, "Bilingual Books for ESL Students . . . and Beyond," *Children and Libraries* 7 (Winter 2009): 42–46.

4
Reaching the Community

It may seem to librarians that everyone must already know about library services and should be jumping on the bandwagon to partake of all we have to offer. The reality is that, while we are passionate about our work, many people don't have a clue about our programs and services. Keep in mind that our work is multifaceted and touches many different parts of our communities, from the education system to businesses and arts and cultural organizations. We must reach further into the community to entice people through our doors. This involves marketing and publicity. Our efforts to provide services may also involve actually taking our programs to the locations where people are already gathering. The concepts that El día de los niños/El día de los libros embraces are beautifully suited to outreach work, both for bringing services to children and their families and for building partnerships that will enhance library services.

Partnerships

No one can do it all! Partners work together, whereas sponsors or funders provide fiscal support but may not be actively involved in the planning and execution of programs. You will want, and probably need, some of both types of supporters. Create a Día team that includes representatives from various areas of your library, such as the circulation desk staff, but that also includes a wide range of community stakeholders. Include representatives from parent organizations, other community organizations, the education community, and service clubs to put together a great program. Some partnerships may be obvious—like the local schools—but look widely and smartly for others who can help the library achieve its goals.

Look for immigrant resources in your community. Agencies and organizations that are already working with immigrant populations may offer access to the populations you want to reach, space for programs, or translation services, or they may bring their services to the library as part of your celebration. Although Spanish speakers and Hispanic or Latino families may be the largest target group for your Día celebration, don't overlook other populations of recent immigrants, including Hmong, Russian, and Somali groups.

Religion is important to many families, so look for churches as partners. The church officials are trusted by the community they serve, so their seal of approval for library activities can help alleviate any fears or concerns parents might have about library services. Churches may be willing to include information about El día de los niños/El día de los libros activities in the newsletter, distribute information during services, or participate in literacy activities at the library's celebration.

Local businesses can provide funding and in-kind resources. They may also help promote your programs by distributing information at the checkout stands, printing library information on paper bags, or providing space for library card sign-ups. Look for businesses that have a common interest in education, children, families, or community service, but don't overlook businesses that employ people from the community you want to reach or that employ people who need to improve their own literacy skills. Some of the biggest supporters of library literacy programs are businesses run by individuals who themselves struggled to get an education or improve their own lives.

Look for internal partners. This category includes other departments within your library but also other departments in your school district, city, or county that may be able to help. This help might include developing graphics for your program or providing giveaway items, printing materials, and website support. Utility departments within a city or county are often very supportive, for example, and law enforcement agencies frequently want to partner to reach the same segments of the community that the library is serving to foster better relationships.

Media outlets, including print news, television stations, and radio stations, are great partners. Be sure to go beyond the mainstream outlets. Visit bodegas and convenience stores in the neighborhoods you want to reach to see what free newspapers and magazines they offer to customers. Look for community radio stations that reach targeted audiences. In many communities, the public television and radio stations are strong supporters of educational projects. Don't overlook social-networking media. Bloggers exist in virtually every niche market and interest, so search them out to spread the word about your Día activities.

Outreach

Many of the children who are already visiting the public library come from middle-class families and may have parents who grew up with libraries. Although we certainly want such children and their families to continue using the library, we can be of greater service by reaching out to children who don't have the opportunity to visit the library on a regular basis. Through outreach efforts, we bring library services and users together. In most cases, our goal is to bring those new users into the library, but in some situations, that may not happen for years. The American Library Association's Office for Literacy and Outreach Services (www.ala.org/ala/aboutala/offices/olos/) offers assistance in identifying and promoting strategies for achieving equitable access to service. Check out its tool kit "Serving Non-English Speakers in U.S. Public Libraries" (www.ala.org/ala/aboutala/offices/olos/toolkits/nonenglishspeakers.cfm) for tips for successful outreach programs and examples of programs from around the country.

Outreach entails both reaching into the community by taking library programs out of the building and creating opportunities for the library, through its staff, to interact with community members. Depending on the specifics of your community, most libraries should combine both types of outreach for a successful Día program. Although it may not be as immediately obvious for school libraries, outreach efforts can be achieved both by partnering with the school library and other organizations and internally, such as by partnering with upper or lower campuses. Remember that students' families are part of the school community, and Día activities provide wonderful opportunities to bring parents and younger siblings into the school library.

If the library is already celebrating Día with events in the library, look for ways to reach out to even more families in the community. If the library has not started a Día program, outreach efforts may be the perfect way to get started.

Marketing and Publicity

You will need to market and publicize your Día program to reach as many people as possible. Marketing positions the library as a place people look to for the services and programs they want. It involves building good customer relations and strengthening relationships with the media, community organizations, and businesses. Marketing is often about the big picture—building the library as a place that welcomes speakers of other languages and that helps families preserve and celebrate their own cultures. It's about attracting people to our locations and enticing them to use our services. Marketing is a process that includes planning and research to ensure that services and programs are reaching the target audience. The process includes working out how you will communicate the services you offer, how you know whether the services are still valid, and whether the services you provide are of the quality demanded by the community.

Publicity and media coverage play an important role in marketing the library to the community. Although you may not have the time to put together a full-blown communications plan, take time to consider how you will promote your program and how you can best reach the community you want to bring into the library. Work up a to-do list and think about where you will have the most impact for the resources you have available.

Publicity is the process of disseminating information to gain public interest. It can include a variety of techniques for getting the word out about your "product." Some publicity efforts require funds to pay for advertising, but there are also a lot of methods that require only some printing and your time. Most libraries already do some publicity, but it may be limited to efforts inside the building.

Keep in mind that it is pretty easy to reach people who are already coming into the library. Not that you won't want to provide flyers, postcards, bookmarks, and such for them, but you will need to put more effort into connecting with the harder to reach members of your community. Your primary target audience for Día celebrations is people who are unaware of the library or unfamiliar with the services offered and with the library's commitment to bilingual and cultural literacy. Step out of your comfort zone to look for partners that can connect you with people who are not already library users. Look for opportunities in the targeted neighborhoods to promote the program.

Publicizing your program both is time intensive and requires a sustained effort over time. Be prepared to overcommunicate your plans. People need to hear a message several times for it to be effective, but they also need to be ready to receive the information. The most successful promotion for your programs usually comes from personal contact, but few of us have the time and resources to do a lot of one-on-one networking. Select publicity activities that will make the most of the resources you have. Think creatively and ask for help from staff and the community. Enlist partners who can help spread the word and invite participants.

One of the most successful venues for reaching families is often the local church, mosque, or synagogue. For many families, their religious leaders have a great deal of credibility, and if the priest, pastor, rabbi, or imam supports the program, people will pay attention. Ask to speak at the beginning of services or to meet and greet people at the end of the services. Many churches and synagogues have newsletters or bulletins and might be willing to advertise Día activities (often you can also purchase advertising for a small fee). Many organizations also host annual festivals of their own, so offer to host a library table or provide an outreach storytime or puppet show. You'll reach a lot of new people!

Check with your local government to find neighborhood associations and other community organizations. Offer to speak at a meeting or ask that publicity be distributed through local newsletters and social-networking sources like Yahoo! groups.

It takes time to hang around public clinics and health-care facilities, but you will reach a lot of members of your target audience by visiting Women, Infants, and Children (WIC) clinics and other community gathering places. Talk about the library and its programs, emphasizing that no costs are involved and that all are welcome.

Ask your local, county, or state government to issue a proclamation in support of Día. Flo Trujillo, of Farmington Public Library, secured a proclamation from the governor of New Mexico. Other states have regularly issued proclamations, and city councils frequently are willing to do this. Proclamations provide an opportunity for

Sample Proclamation

PROCLAMATION

[Insert name of city, county, or other jurisdiction.]

Whereas, Literacy is defined as the foundation of learning and is essential to the growth and success of all children;

Whereas, Many of the nations of the world celebrate *Children's Day* in recognition and celebration of children, the future of our country;

Whereas, Children represent the hopes and dreams of [insert jurisdiction];

Whereas, Children are the center of most families;

Whereas, The importance of reading and education are most often communicated through family members and supported by such public institutions as the [insert name of library] and its literacy programs;

Whereas, Children are the responsibility of all citizens, and all citizens should be encouraged to celebrate the gift that children are to our society;

Now, therefore, be it proclaimed by the [insert offices and/or names of the group issuing the proclamation] that [insert date for the celebration] shall be known as:

"El día de los niños/El día de los libros"

and we urge the people of [insert jurisdiction] to join with all children, families, organizations, businesses, and clubs to observe El día de los niños/ El día de los libros with appropriate activities.

In Witness Whereof, I have hereunto set my hand and caused the official seal of [insert name of jurisdiction] *to be affixed this* [insert day] *day of* [insert month and year].

Signature of Official

you to take your message about bilingual literacy to a wider audience. Display a copy of the signed proclamation in the library to attract attention and add to the significance of your programming.

Other places to post or distribute information include the following:

- family restaurants and pizza parlors
- farmers' markets
- Head Start centers and child-care centers
- laundromats and dry-cleaning stores
- local grocery stores, especially smaller bodegas and convenience stores that serve ethnic communities
- recreation centers
- sports facilities
- the mall
- thrift shops and neighborhood shops

The opportunities are endless, but look for places where the people you are trying to reach congregate or visit on a regular basis. This may involve a little detective work, so be sure to ask for suggestions from members of the community you are trying to reach.

Consider hosting a library Día table at the local farmers' market. People often take a more leisurely pace at markets and view the experience as entertainment in addition to a shopping excursion. Take part in community fairs, festivals, and events, even if all you can do is put flyers in packets or hand out bookmarks. Being visible in the community is part of building essential relationships, and you may meet some potential volunteers or partners.

Postcards can be an effective direct-mail tool. As part of its promotional materials, California's San Francisco Public Library prepared a postcard that provided basic information about the Día event and its sponsors. Partner groups and the library were able to send these out to constituents and make them available in-house. Postcards are also much less expensive to print than you might expect. If you don't have local access to a low-cost printer, check out online printers like VistaPrint (www.vistaprint.com) or GotPrint (www.gotprint.com) to buy a thousand or more postcards for less than $100.

It's also important that you include every member of the staff and all of your library volunteers in the promotion of Día. Provide them with talking points—the message you want them to share—so that they are prepared to promote the program when they engage with patrons or when they are out in the community.

Using the Media

Working with the media involves some special skills and can be a challenging part of your efforts to market the library and your Día program. Opportunities for working with the media include print resources, like local newspapers and magazines, as

The Texas State Library's Día logo, available to all libraries

The official Día logo, available from ALSC

The California State Library's Día logo, available free online

well as radio and television. The media can also include online resources like blogs and electronic newsletters.

For your Día program, consider developing a logo and a tagline or slogan that can be used to identify the program. Often local advertising firms can help with pro bono services, or a local college or university marketing class may be able to help. The logo can be used in print media and on items prepared for distribution by the library. It brands your project and makes any activities immediately identifiable as a Día event. The official logo includes the April 30 date, but feel free to adapt it to remove or change the date. It is available from the Association for Library Service to Children (www.ala.org/ala/mgrps/divs/alsc/initiatives/diadelosninos/diaresources/dialogos.cfm). Other supporters have created other images, most of which libraries can use. The Texas State Library has a logo, created and donated by James W. Larson for use by any library, available online (www.tsl.state.tx.us/ld/projects/ninos/) that resembles *papel picado*, a Mexican cut-paper craft. The California State Library offers a logo online (www.diacalifornia.org/graphics.html) that simply indicates April as the month for Día.

A tagline is an advertising tool that sums up your brand and the personality of your program in a few catchy, memorable words. The tagline should be short and to the point. It should be something that you can use over and over again, as you will hear it a lot. Taglines are very useful in print media but also for broadcast opportunities, when you may only have sixty or ninety seconds to get your message out and want something memorable to make your point. Examples of taglines include "@ your library," "Something for everyone," "Reading matters," and "Read for life."

Print Media

Publicity through print media can include press releases, paid and unpaid advertising, stories, and photographs. For Día activities, be sure that you look around your community for newspapers and magazines that reach your intended audience. This may mean that you have to go to a convenience store in the community and look for the periodicals that are sold or given away free there. You can also look for local media in online resources like Newslink (www.newslink.org) or ABYZ News Links (www.abyznewslinks.com/about.htm). Be aware, however, that these sites include only a few ethnic newspapers (and those that are may be listed as "specialty" or be difficult to locate). If your town is too small to have specialty newspapers, look in the largest city near you.

Don't overlook smaller newspapers and specialty papers, like the *Greensheet* or the *Nickel Saver*. Especially in larger communities, these media outlets may welcome your publicity, and their readership may reach new markets for the library. Other helpful alternatives to consider are local business newspapers, college publications, and publications aimed at older adults. Often grandparents will be the ones taking grandchildren to community events.

Ads can be public service listings or paid placements. Paid placements, of course, mean that you have total control over when and where the ad runs, but the costs often take this option out of the library's plans. Media partners can help with your planning, but you want your ads to run early and often. Depending on the extent of your program, begin advertising about a month out, and repeat the ads at least a week and a day before the start. Remember that monthly publications need material six to eight weeks before the month of publication, so if your Día event will be held at the end of April, you may need to submit publicity as early as February 1. That publicity can be very broad and direct patrons to the library's website and telephone contact.

Press Releases

Press releases follow a standard format. For most media outlets, they do not need to be elaborate. Most community newspaper editors want "just the facts." Press releases must, however, include enough information to attract interest and sound newsworthy. What you write may encourage the editor to assign a reporter to cover your program, in which case the reporter will call for more details. In larger communities, the newspaper may list only the basic facts. Follow these tips for successful press releases:

- Use simple sentences, straightforward language, and short paragraphs.
- Put the most important information first, and include additional information further into the press release, to be used if space permits.

Sample Press Release

FOR IMMEDIATE RELEASE

Contact:
[Provide a contact name, telephone number, and e-mail address]

Celebrate bilingual literacy at the Diverse City Library

Diverse City, April 2, 2011—The Diverse City Library is hosting a free program to celebrate El día de los niños/El día de los libros on Saturday, April 30, 2011, from 11:00 a.m. until 3:00 p.m. This daylong celebration supports the library's family literacy initiative and is the culmination of a daily commitment to link children and books.

Programs, beginning at 11:00 a.m., will feature local children's authors, storytellers, a multilingual puppet show, music, food, and crafts. [**Add details about the performers and presenters.**] Bilingual literacy and an appreciation for all of the languages spoken in our community is "important for a child's educational and personal achievement and enhances global awareness by linking all children to books, languages, and cultures," according to the library's director, Di Verse. "We want all families to enjoy the literary heritage of the world's great cultures through the books and stories available at the library."

Support for the program has been provided by [**include names of contributors and sponsors**]. The program is open to children of all ages and their families. For more information, and a specific schedule of events, check the library's website, www.diversecitylibrary.com, or call 555-1234.

- Accuracy is important! Double-check spelling and grammar, the date and time of the event, the address, and the phone number. Ask someone to proofread your press release.
- Limit the release to one page or less.
- Attach a program flyer, if available, to your press release.
- Include contact information so the media will know how to reach the program director for more information or how to cover your program in more detail.
- The first paragraph of a press release is the lede, and it sets the stage for the message. Make the point quickly, and grab the readers' attention!
- Add details in the next paragraph and, if possible, include a human-interest angle or a quote. It is appropriate to "put words" in your director's mouth by providing a quote.
- Provide contact information for those who want to know more about the event.
- Add a headline at the top; date the press release; and if the information is for immediate publication, say so. "Embargoed" press releases request that the information not be published before a certain date, but most libraries do not need to delay publication of information.

In some communities, the local papers welcome guest articles and will run an article that you write. Often they will also run photographs that you take and submit. Radio stations reach a lot of people, often when they are something of a captive audience in their cars. Check out Newslink (www.newslink.org) and ABYZ News Links (www.abyznewslinks.com/about.htm) for some of the cultural and non-English-language stations in your area, but keep in mind that not all are listed.

It is absolutely essential that publicity be prepared in the languages represented in your community. Look for community partners and volunteers who can help with accurate and appropriate translations. Spanish has different nuances and vocabulary among the various Spanish-speaking peoples, so if your community is predominantly Cuban, for example, be sure the translator is conversant in that form of Spanish. The same is true for many other spoken languages; regional dialects may seem to separate a culture more than the language joins the people, and people in the Chinese or Indian community may speak one or more of several languages that are prevalent in their country of origin. Although some differences are major, dialect differences may be more of an issue in spoken language. Still, be careful when translating written material, because idioms and slang can greatly change your meaning!

Measuring Success

As you plan your El día de los niños/El día de los libros programs and activities, it's also important to consider how you will know if you accomplish what you set out to do. Begin by establishing some goals, as discussed in chapter 1 of this book. Look at the mission statements and goals for El día de los niños/El día de los libros, and restructure them to meet the priorities of your program.

Traditionally, programs are measured on the basis of program inputs, activities, and outputs—what resources were available for the program; what you did with the resources; and what happened, including how many people attended and how many items were distributed or used by attendees. Theoretically, it is considered desirable to have more resources (money, staff, volunteers, and materials) and do more things so that more people participate by attending programs and borrowing or using materials. Often we measure success by looking at how much these factors increased over the previous program, and these measures do give us a snapshot of how things went.

Although attendance and participation are frequently considered the ultimate measure of success, and we all like to see our efforts result in high numbers, outputs are only one aspect of success. More often these days libraries and other nonprofits are evaluating how well the programs and activities served the community. We are looking at what difference the programs made to the targeted audience. To do this, we look at whether the library is doing a good job in reaching the different demographics in the community. We ask whether new communities are coming to the library's programs and whether new families are using other library services. For example, are books being taken from displays when they include books and materials in languages other than English? The United Way developed outcomes-based evaluation, which many libraries use to evaluate their work. The Institute for Museum and Library Services (IMLS), the federal agency that oversees federal library funding, also encourages the use of outcomes-based evaluation as a tool. For more information on using outcomes-based evaluation in libraries, see the IMLS resources at the institute's website (www.imls.gov/applicants/obe.shtm).

Simply put, outcomes-based evaluation looks at the impact of the services on our patrons. It tries to look at the difference our programs are making in people's lives. Did our services change someone's behavior or attitude? Did the participants do something differently because of the library's program? We find out much of this feedback by requesting it from attendees. This can be in the form of surveys and questionnaires, but librarians can also ask for comments from participants for use in reports, grant applications, letters to sponsors, and publicity for the next year.

For multicultural programming, it can also be helpful to set cultural competency goals for the library. These can be short-term activities that build community relationships or foster ties to cultures not currently part of your Día activities, and that move library services closer to being all-inclusive and inviting to groups that may not currently feel comfortable using the library.

5
Programming—
Celebrating Día in Public Libraries

Getting Started

Before you begin to plan your Día programs, be sure that you know what you want to do, have established a planning outline, and have a high level of institutional support. Although additional approvals may not be necessary if you are simply integrating Día activities into an ongoing storytime or other basic programming, be sure to let your supervisor know what you are doing and why. This is essential for support as you expand and enhance programming and will be required if you need additional budget resources.

Does the library director understand the need to promote bilingualism? If you are in a school library, does the principal support bilingual education? Do teachers appreciate that reading in one language supports reading in a second or third language? Does the library staff truly support the ideas of diversity? What resources—staff, funds, interdepartmental cooperation—are available to you? Can you find additional resources and establish partnerships to support El día de los niños/El día de los libros programming? You need support for the programs to succeed, or at least you need to know where you may not have support so that you can find other avenues to achieve your goals. The best-planned program can fail to meet expectations if the marketing person is not on board and doesn't send out the publicity!

When planning your program, involve the community from the beginning. Don't start with preconceptions about what you can or cannot do. Also, as several librarians have pointed out in conversations about multicultural programming, don't assume that you know everything about a culture even if you are part of that cultural group or feel you are pretty familiar with the people and their beliefs. One of the most exciting things about being a children's librarian is that we have new opportunities to reach new audiences all of the time. Because few of us speak languages other than English or may speak only one additional language, community involvement will be important to the success of the programs. Begin cultivating support for El día de los niños/El día de los libros every day, all year round. Talk to parents who indicate that they speak another language or who are from other cultures. Most people are eager to share their language and culture.

Invite potential partners and supporters to a brainstorming session. Be prepared to give a brief overview of Día, and recognize that some bilingual activities may already be taking place in the community. Acknowledge that the program may begin small and grow over time. Also recognize that some potential partners may be concerned about funding. It's important in planning any project to assure people that if they can't participate now, they will be welcome later. Accept that it may take time to build relationships with community partners. Remember also that partnerships may not be completely equal; each partner must find benefit for its own organization. Be open to ideas, even if you think they are not practical or may not be doable the first year. Record them to review again later. The craziest-sounding idea now may be the best idea later! As you hear ideas and begin to refine them, look for ways to link activities back to the fundamentals of Día—bilingual literacy, language skills, and reading!

Identify Community Needs

People are more alike than they are different, but each community has its own unique needs and responds differently to different activities. Although the broader target for your Día program will be all children in the community, consider the needs and interests of the specific group or groups you are trying to reach. Programs that include elements of cultural authenticity and that are culturally relevant will have better success in reaching your target audience.

In a survey of libraries serving multicultural populations conducted in 2010 by the Association for Library Service to Children, more than 55 percent of respondents reported that there were cultural or ethnic groups in their community that were underserved (the library reached a small percentage of that population) or unserved (the library reached virtually no one from that population). Almost as startling was the revelation that more than a quarter of the respondents didn't know whether there were underserved or unserved cultural groups. In your community, the U.S. Census can help identify areas of the community in which people speak a language other than English at home. Check out American Fact Finder (http://factfinder .census.gov/home/saff/main.html) for data and maps. The school district can also often help in identifying languages spoken at home. But ultimately it is important to go to the community. Look for stores and churches that serve your target audiences. Identify key leaders in those communities and ask for their help. Most will support your efforts to enhance bilingual literacy.

According to the Hispanic Scholarship Fund, 90 percent of Hispanic parents believe that education, especially a college degree, is a key factor to enjoying a better life. Helping their children get a good education is a key need in most communities, and Día activities support that effort from the beginnings of a child's life.

What Can You Do for Día?

Begin by identifying the cultural groups in your community. This may be relatively easier to do in some communities than in others, but it can always be done. Look for cultural or ethnic chambers of commerce. Check the phone book or the religious listings in the local newspaper for churches that serve the communities you want to reach. Ask the school district what languages other than English are spoken by families with children in the school system. The state may have an office that works with cultural affairs that can provide information about organizations in your community that could be potential partners. Talk with social services agencies, especially those that serve young children and families. Drive around neighborhoods to look for grocery stores that cater to immigrant and cultural communities.

Start small. Many libraries have found that consistency and a slow buildup of Día programs is critical to success. You can always add partners, increase the number of activities, or add locations for programs as the project grows, but it can be very hard to overcome the results of a poorly planned, understaffed event. Figure out who will run the program, what presenters will be needed, and who you hope your audience will be. In many ways, the questions you need to think about are the 5 *W*s of journalism: Who? What? Where? Why? When?

- Whom do you hope to reach with your program?
- Who will be involved?
- What will the program entail?
- What are you going to do during the program?
- What resources do you need?
- Where will you hold the program?
- Where will you advertise?
- Why are you doing what you are doing?
- Why should anyone want to come to the program?
- When (date and time) will you hold the program?
- When do things need to be ready?

Ideally, Día activities support reading every day, regularly and consistently, and continued use of the library and support for education. However, Día isn't built in a day! Many libraries start with a community event on or around April 30 and build out from there. Do what makes sense and is achievable for you now and then build on your success.

Many libraries use Día as a way to kick off summer-reading activities and promote specific programs that encourage children to continue reading during the school break. Día can also be used as the kickoff for other programs that you are highlighting in the library. Remember that the concepts are simple and flexible.

Invite members of the community to help with the planning and with the programming. A huge part of building community support for Día and other library programs is networking and being open to the community. Listen for people speaking with accents. Ask them what language they speak and whether they are interested in sharing their language with children. Most people won't turn you down, and those who do usually only do so because of scheduling conflicts. In fact, many who turn down your request will offer to find a substitute. Also check with local universities that may have foreign students. In Austin, Texas, many of the mothers of storytime participants at the branch closest to the university are the spouses of foreign students, and they are eager to work with the library. Adrienne Ehlert Bashista, former media specialist for the Virginia Cross Elementary School in Siler City, North Carolina, found that parents were quite willing to help out in the library and were delighted that they could help even though their own English-language skills were very limited. Either English was not necessary for the volunteer work, or it was those very skills in other languages that made them most valuable!

As the children's librarian, you are cultivating support all of the time and looking for opportunities to celebrate or highlight other cultures and languages throughout the year. This helps to get things ready for a big annual celebration of El día de los niños/El día de los libros.

As you consider when to hold your program, consider whether this will be a onetime event or whether it will be ongoing over a period of time. Consider the audience and your community. In some communities, Sunday is a poor choice because of church activities or because the library is normally closed on that day. However Kenton County (Kentucky) Public Library enjoyed great success with Sunday programming, and the library meeting rooms needed for a big event were not taken up by other programs on that day. Working families won't be able to come to programs held in the middle of the day, but they may come for an evening storytime and special event. Consider also what else is happening in the community. Spring can be filled with major outdoor festivals, especially in communities that are welcoming relief from a cold winter. That may create a lot of competition for a full-day outdoor extravaganza. Even if you decide that a particular day is the best (or only) day for your events, you should know about other events with which you are competing. Although the official date for El día de los niños/El día de los libros is April 30, you can use any day for your major celebration. There is no right or wrong answer—there is the answer for your community.

What Can You Afford to Do for Día?
Budgeting

Before you begin to decide what you can do, you need to establish a budget and have a firm grasp of what various functions will cost. Some items will already be included in the library's budget. For example, if you decide to host a series of world languages storytimes, this may not cost anything more than the staff time that is already dedicated to planning and presenting storytimes. The budget may be a simple listing of what you would like to fund with estimated costs or it may be very detailed. Regardless of whether you will seek partnerships and sponsors or solicit in-kind donations, you need to know what your Día programming will cost. Be prepared, if at all possible, to offer a small stipend or honorarium to the people who present at the program. Even $25 shows that you value people's skills and appreciate their help. It also helps to pay for gas and lunch! To determine the true cost of a program, some libraries also like to include staff costs and the value of typical office supplies that will be used, even though these items may already be on hand. Although some of the line items listed here won't be applicable to smaller celebrations, it is surprisingly easy to overlook needed resources until you are further into the planning process!

Items to include in the budget, as applicable:

- advertising (cost for paid radio, television, print ads)
- books or CDs for sale (to be autographed by authors and performers)
- craft supplies
- fees for authors, speakers, storytellers, performers, and presenters
- giveaway items (books, special bookmarks, stickers, wristbands)
- honoraria or stipends for nonprofessional presenters
- material for the collection (special purchases to support the Día program)
- office supplies
- photocopying
- postage
- printing costs (for flyers, bookmarks, posters, postcards, certificates)
- refreshments
- rental of audiovisual equipment (amplifiers and sound systems for presenters)
- rental of chairs and tables
- rental of tents or canopies (for outdoor programs)
- temporary staffing (janitorial, security, parking lot attendants)
- professional services (website support, logo development, graphic artists)
- travel for presenters (mileage, airfare, hotel, meals)

Funding

Ideally, the library budget would support all of the Día program costs. The reality is that you will probably have to seek additional funding, and this can be a great way to enhance partnerships and community outreach:

- Look to Friends of the Library or the parent-teacher association in the local schools.
- Local businesses can often offer funding and in-kind support. Many national businesses, like insurance companies and realty agencies, have community giving programs that allow local offices to make small contributions (usually less than $500) to support community programs and projects.
- Look for grants. Check out blogs like *Library Grants* (http://librarygrants .blogspot.com) for ongoing opportunities. Look locally for grant help. The Council on Foundations' Community Foundation Locator (www.cof.org/ whoweserve/community/resources/index.cfm?navItemNumber=15626# locator) can help you find resources in your community.
- Look for grants from library-related organizations. California and Texas have offered grants to libraries in their states through the California State Library and the Texas Library Association. Local chapters of REFORMA have offered minigrants. The Ezra Jack Keats Foundation (www.ezra-jack -keats.org) offers minigrants for programming that is compatible with Día activities. The grants may not be available every year, but keep an eye out for them.
- Seek support from local media. In addition to offering in-kind support for advertising, they may have funds to help promote literacy. For example, some public television stations have early literacy initiatives that can provide books for giveaways or help with character costumes and items for goody bags.
- Seek support from bookstores. Bookstores have a vested interest in a literate community and many, like Half-Price Books, are valued partners in providing free books for library programs.
- Organizations like First Book (www.firstbook.org) can help libraries provide low-cost, high-quality books to children. They provide a supply of books free or at greatly reduced prices to low-income communities. Other potential partners for books to distribute include Reading Is Fundamental (www.rif.org) and local public television stations.
- Be sure to check with local government offices and other agencies. In El Paso, Texas, the local Mexican consulate is able to provide free books in Spanish.

Two main things to remember in seeking funds are to start early and to not be afraid to ask for what you need. Be direct in your request, and ask the potential funder or donor what they need from you. Be prepared to explain succinctly what you are doing, why it is important, and how your request will benefit the funder.

Ideas for Día Celebration Programs

Remember that the goal is to promote and advocate for multicultural and bilingual literacy and bookjoy every day. However, in practice, your Día celebration will probably consist of a number of program components throughout the year that may culminate in a major celebration of reading and cultural literacy. It's prudent and reasonable to begin small and to develop a network of programs and activities that link together to become your Día celebration.

Although each library will design its own programming based on local opportunities and constraints, it can be helpful to have templates that assist you in organizing your festivities. These templates are based on programs from a variety of different libraries, but you can easily adapt them to your specific needs and opportunities. Link several programs together throughout the year to achieve year-round Día programming.

Bilingual Storytimes

Storytimes are the foundation of children's services in most public libraries, and they are becoming an important part of early literacy activities in school libraries, especially for those that reach out to preschool children. Use your experience with storytimes to create a Spanish-language (or other-language) storytime, a bilingual storytime, or a world-languages storytime.

Storytime is the foundation program for many libraries, including school libraries, and is often the first point of entry for Día programming. Clearly, it would be best if a fluent speaker of the language could conduct the storytime, but that is not always possible and is not a major stumbling block.

Bilingual storytimes provide a great opportunity for partnering with another group, especially if the librarian is not conversant in the second language. The English-speaking librarian can read a story in English while a volunteer or community partner reads the story in the second language. Most people are willing to help if you ask them. Fluent speakers help to bring an authentic tone to the stories and help to attract both families from the cultures and families from the broader community. The partner need only be willing to put in a little preparation time, reading the book a few times ahead of the program, and to read the book during the program. Ideally the partner would also be willing to help promote the program and assist with other aspects of the program, including recommending appropriate enhancements, such as crafts and refreshments.

There are several popular books, like *Farmer Duck*, by Martin Waddell, and *Splash!* by Flora McDonnell, that are available in multiple languages. Read the story first in English, and then at each storytime, share the same book in a different language. This provides consistency for the children, who know the story and can follow along in whatever language is being used that day while being exposed to another language. *Lulu Loves the Library*, by Anna McQuinn, is another great book to use. Published in the United States as *Lola at the Library*, the story features a black child who discovers that the library is a fun place. A new paperback edition includes a multilanguage CD with the story in English, Welsh, Irish, French, Polish, Italian, Turkish, Gujarati, Urdu, Ndebele, Luganda, Igbo, Arabic, Somali, Amharic, Tigrinya, Portuguese, Spanish, and Mandarin. A book like *The Drum Calls Softly*, by David Bouchard and Shelley Willier, is bilingual, in English and Cree, but is also available in French. As an added bonus, the book, which is about a community round dance, includes a CD with recitations of the text in both English and Cree and accompanying round-dance drumming.

If you have trouble finding copies of books in other languages from your regular book wholesale suppliers or jobbers (Baker and Taylor or Ingram, for example), try an online retailer like Language Lizard (www.languagelizard.com), which also sells copies of standard fairy tales in multiple languages. Not every book has to be in the language of the cultures on which you are focusing the storytime. Not many books include Hmong language, but you can supplement a book like *Nine-in-One, Grr! Grr! A Folktale from the Hmong People of Laos*, by Blia Xiong, with a song or rhyme in the language.

Often the authors of books that could be used in a world-language program provide resources on their websites. For example, Grace Lin's website (www .gracelin.com) provides a script for a theatrical adaptation of *The Ugly Vegetables* that elementary school children could perform for preschoolers. Lin also offers files that play the pronunciation of Chinese words and show the characters for the vegetables included in her book. The Utah State Library has made scripts for bilingual Spanish storytimes available online (http://library.utah.gov/programs/ spanish/Scripts.html). Supported by REFORMA of Utah, the scripts focus on popular themes and offer book ideas, rhymes, songs, and more in both English and Spanish. Two additional resources for planning Spanish-language storytimes are *Read Me a Rhyme in Spanish and English/Léame una rima en español e inglés*, by Rose Zertuche Treviño, which offers templates for storytimes for various age groups, and *Early Literacy Programming en español: Mother Goose on the Loose Programs for Bilingual Learners*, by Betsy Diamant-Cohen, which includes a CD with sixty-five songs to support bilingual programs.

Library resources like Treviño's *Read Me a Rhyme in Spanish and English* provide filler rhymes in both English and Spanish, along with books and crafts that can be used in storytimes for children from infants through school age. Although it is perhaps easiest for librarians to find rhymes and other resources for Spanish-language storytimes, rhymes and songs are available in every language. Try *Skip across the Ocean: Nursery Rhymes from around the World*, collected by Floella Benjamin, for action rhymes and songs from other countries. Some rhymes appear in both English and the original language. *Children's Songs from Afghanistan*, by Louise M. Pascale, includes a CD with sixty minutes' worth of songs. The illustrated book, available through the Folk Arts Center of New England, includes lyrics in Farsi, Pashto, and Uzbek, along with English translations and transliterations, plus the musical notation for each song. Look to publishers like Tuttle (http:// peripublishinggroup.com/tuttle/) for material in Asian languages.

Italy has a rich legacy of traditional nursery rhymes that are much more varied than the Anglo-Saxon body of rhymes. According to Lella Gandini and Simonetta Sambrotta, in a 2002 article in *The Lion and the Unicorn*, "The terms most commonly used today are: ninne nanne, nenie or cantilene (lullabies or singsongs), when they are intended to make a baby go to sleep; tiritere and filastrocche (nursery rhymes), when they are used by adults to entertain children; conte and filastrocche (counting rhymes), for pieces invented by children and used to count out, jump rope or as part of their games."[1] There are also many regional variations to nursery rhymes, so don't be surprised if a native speaker of Italian communicates a rhyme differently. Use a rhyme like "Pio Pio," a traditional Italian nursery song provided here, as part of a bilingual storytime:

Pio Pio	**Pio Pio**
Pio pio	Pio pio
pio pio.	pio pio.
Il pulcino sono io.	I am the chick.
La mia mamma	My mother
è la chioccia	is the hen
e io vivo nel pollaio.	and I live in the chicken run.
Quando andiamo	When we go
a far la nanna	to sleep
sotto le ali della mamma,	under mommy's wings,
noi dormiamo tranquillamente	we sleep quietly
e la volpe non ci fa niente.	and the fox doesn't harm us.[2]

In India, rhymes are available in several different languages. You can view a video from a Bollywood film on YouTube (www.youtube.com/watch?v=eRi7TzmZsrk) of the following traditional Hindi rhyme:

Chandaa Maama Door Ke	**Uncle Moon**
Chandaa maama door ke,	Uncle Moon far far away,
puye pakaayen boor ke	baking yummy treats
aap khaayen thaali mein,	Eats in a big plate himself,
munne ko den pyaali mein	gives baby a small bowl
chandaa maama door ke,	to eat in
puye pakaayen boor ke	Small bowl breaks,
pyaali gayi toot munnaa gayaa rooth	baby is mad
laayenge nayi pyaaliyaan bajaa bajaa ke	We'll bring new bowls and clap
taaliyaan	our hands
munne ko manaayenge ham doodh	We'll bring a smile to baby's face
malaayi khaayenge,	and will eat treats together
chandaa maama door ke,	Uncle Moon far far away,
puye pakaayen boor ke	baking yummy treats

aap khaayen thaali mein,
    munne ko den pyaali mein
chandaa maama door ke,
    puye pakaayen boor ke

Eats in a big plate himself,
    gives baby a small bowl to eat in
Uncle Moon far far away,
    baking yummy treats[3]

Other Book Sources for Rhymes

The Bilingual Book of Rhymes, Songs, Stories, and Fingerplays, by Pam Schiller, Rafael Lara-Alecio, and Beverly J. Irby

Chinese and English Nursery Rhymes: Share and Sing in Two Languages, by Faye-Lynn Wu

Chinese Mother Goose Rhymes, by Robert Wyndham

Come Out and Play: Count around the World in Five Languages, by Diane Law

Lullabies, Lyrics and Gallows Songs, by Christian Morgenstern

My Little Book of Chinese Words, by Catherine Louis, Mary Chris Bradley, and Bo Shi

My Village: Rhymes from around the World, by Danielle Wright

Rhymes round the World, by Kay Chorao

Sleep Rhymes around the World, by Jane Yolen

Street Rhymes around the World, by Jane Yolen

Tūtū Nēnē: The Hawaiian Mother Goose Rhymes (with mini-CD), by Debra Ryll

Un deux trois: First French Rhymes, by Opal Dunn

Web Sources for Rhymes and Songs

Desi Nursery Rhymes | *www.desinurseryrhymes.com*
This blog was created as a place for a new mother to collect and share Indian and Pakistani nursery rhymes. Some have been translated into English.

India Parenting | *www.indiaparenting.com/rhymes/*
This site is a storehouse of information for parents and includes a database of regional and national rhymes and songs.

Infanzia | *www.infanzia.com/divertiamoci/*
This Italian website provides songs (*canzoni*), lullabies, and rhymes (*filastrocche* and *ninne nanne*), with sound files for some.

It's a Small World | *www.itsasmallworld.co.nz*
A companion site for Danielle Wright's *My Village: Rhymes from around the World*, this website collects rhymes from around the world.

Mama Lisa's World | *www.mamalisa.com*
This website aims to give people a sense of the nursery rhymes and songs sung by or to children in cultures around the world. Click on a continent to find words, and sometimes a video or music file, for songs from many countries.

It's also possible to use audio recordings, some of them enhanced with books that provide the words, of nursery rhymes and song. Try *Dream Songs Night Songs from Mali to Louisiana* (Secret Mountain, 2006) or *Dreamland: World Lullabies and Soothing Songs* (Putumayo, 2003) for soothing songs in languages other than English. One of the most intriguing audio collections is *Lullabies from the Axis of Evil*, which features songs from Afghanistan, Iran, Iraq, North Korea, and other countries (Harmony Ridge Music, 2004).

Producers like Putumayo (www.putumayo.com) sell CDs with music from around the world, often in the language of the country of origin. Putumayo's website frequently provides lyric sheets in the original language with English translations and short video flash-card clips.

Resources for World Language Music

Baby Einstein World Music, by various artists (Buena Vista, 2009)

Chanda Mama Door Ke, by Alaka (Amrit Vani, [2006?])

Gift of the Tortoise, by Ladysmith Black Mambazo (Music for Little People, 1994)

Mediterranean Lullaby, by various artists (Ellipsis Arts, 2000)

Rough Guide to African Music for Children, by various artists (World Music Network, 2005)

Songs in French for Children, by Lucienne Vernay (Sony, 2001)

World Music for Little Ears: Authentic Lullabies from around the World, by various artists (Ellipsis Arts, 2000)

World Party, by various artists (Music for Little People, 2003)

World Playground, by various artists (Putumayo, 1999)

Afterschool and Summer Programs

Afterschool and summer programs, or special programs in public libraries, are generally planned to last about sixty or ninety minutes and are designed for school-age children who may come to the library on their own. Children are pretty independent at this age. You might begin the program by reading a book that is bilingual or dual language, or by sharing a book based in another culture. You might share a chapter from a longer book, or transform it into a puppet show, reader's theater script, or choral reading. Provide another activity (a few possibilities are listed here) and close with a movement activity, short craft, snacks, or a take-home item. Be sure to always display related books and library resources to encourage the joy of reading.

Program elements might include the following:

- author presentations
- book clubs
- crafts
- magic shows
- musicians and singers
- puppetry
- snacks
- special guests
- storytellers

Program: Play with Me

Opening Activity: Learn to say a few words like *hello* and *friend* in a couple of languages. Copy the words onto poster board or a whiteboard so that the participants can join in saying them. Check a book like *Say Hello!* by Rachel Isadora, for help in translations or use the book as an opening read aloud.

Book: *Join Hands!* by Pat Mora
Children of most ages can appreciate this book, and it serves as an excellent start to a program about games that are played in other cultures. It's interesting to see how many games have similarities among cultures, yet each may have its own local twist. Invite special guests to demonstrate how commonly known games like jump rope, hopscotch, or marbles are played by children in their country.

Additional Books:

***Dominoes around the World,* by Mary Lankford.** With its counterpart books *Hopscotch around the World* and *Jacks around the World*, this book looks at cultural variations of a popular game and explains the cultural origins of each variation.

The library *lotería* game, similar to bingo

The *bibliotecaria* (librarian) card from library *lotería*

Kids around the World Play! **by Arlette Braman.** Learn about fun and games children play around the world. Entries include a brief history of each game, cultural links, and instructions and patterns for making your own games and toys.

Playing lotería/El juego de la lotería, **by René Colato Laínez.** A young boy visits his grandmother in Mexico and learns to play *la lotería*, a game much like bingo.

Stretcher Activity: Although the age group for the program will be far beyond the typical fingerplay stretchers, the use of hand rhymes, jump-rope songs, and other elementary school games can provide an opportunity to share another language. Extend the languages included in your program by incorporating music, CDs, and video or DVDs. Let's Go Guang! (www.ahachinese.com) is a bilingual series designed to help children learn Chinese. Short, animated stories feature words in Mandarin, Pinyin, and simplified Chinese and songs to help children learn the language. The DVD is available alone or in a multimedia kit that includes a book and flash cards, as well as an educator guide. Teach Me Tapes (www.teachmetapes. com) is another producer that sells CDs with music in several different languages that teach the language through songs. An example of a popular traditional action song and its translation follows. During the song, players tap their fists on top of each other, right on left, then left on right, as they say the words to the rhyme:

One Potato, Two Potato (*traditional*)
One potato, two potato, three
 potato, four.
Five potato, six potato, seven
 potato, more!
Eight potato, nine potato,
Now we count to ten.
Let's say the rhyme all over again.

Una papa, dos papas
Una papa, dos papas, tres
 papas, cuatro.
Cinco papas, seis papas, siete
 papas. ¡Más!
Ocho papas, nueve papas,
Y ahora contaremos hasta diez.
Repetiremos la rima otra vez.[4]

Activity: People around the world play dominoes, a game that has its origins in China. Purchase several inexpensive domino sets and let the children try several of the versions described in Lankford's book. If you don't have a copy of *Dominoes around the World*, share some of the versions from the website Domino Plaza (www .xs4all.nl/~spaanszt/Domino_Plaza.html).

Robert Esparza, a staff member with the San Mateo County (California) Library, developed art for a librarian *lotería* game, a version of the traditional Mexican game that is similar to bingo. Pair playing this game with a reading of *Playing lotería*, by René Colato Laínez.

Craft: Mancala

Mancala is a basic type of board game that originated in Africa but is played in some version around the world. Archeologists have found remnants of mancala game boards dating back to the sixth century. The object of the game is to capture more play pieces than the other player.

A mancala game made from egg cartons and small fruits

Materials: Empty egg cartons (one per child); scissors; dried beans, candies, small fruits, marbles, large beads, small buttons, or other small items to use as tokens (forty-eight per child); glue

Directions: Cut the top off the egg carton. Then cut the top in half across the middle. Glue each half underneath a section of four cups, allowing about half of the piece to stick out from the ends to create trays. Place four tokens in each of the twelve cups. If desired, additional craft supplies can be provided so that the children can paint or decorate their game board.

The game is played by two players. Place the game on a table lengthwise between the players. Each "owns" the tray to the player's right and the six cups on his or her side of the board. The first player scoops up the tokens from any one of his cups and begins dropping a single token into each cup to his right, working counterclockwise until all of the pieces are gone. When the player reaches his own tray, he drops a piece there before continuing into the opposing player's cups. If the player reaches the opposing player's tray, it is skipped. When the player runs out of tokens, the other player takes a turn. Play continues to alternate between players until all of the tokens are gone from the cups. Players then count the tokens in their own trays and the player with the most wins. There are many variations to the game, so encourage the children to look for other rules in books or on the Internet.

Websites

How to Say In | *www.howtosayin.com/friend.html*
This website provides a translation for the word *friend* in several major languages.

TOPICS Online Magazine | *www.topics-mag.com/edition11/games-section.htm*
This publication offers learners of English a place to publish their ideas for an online audience. The games section describes and provides pictures of children's games, ranging from hopscotch and jump rope to tops and marbles, played in other countries.

WikiHow | *www.wikihow.com/Say-Hello-in-Different-Languages*
This site gives greetings in many of the world's nearly three thousand languages.

Half-Day Programs

Half-day programs may last two to three hours. They generally offer multiple opportunities for children and families to participate in a variety of activities. Because of the length of the program, families may stay for all or part of the program, so it is important to have self-contained elements that can be completed in a shorter time period and that are not dependent on attending the entire time. It is also a good idea to provide some breaks. Providing a distinct break about halfway through the program also allows families to leave if necessary without feeling that they are disrupting the program. A good mix of activities allows the children to move from element to element, and transitions allow the children to stand and move between activities or stations.

The example provided here is adapted from a program developed by Ramarie Beaver at the Plano (Texas) Public Library. The program focused on multiple countries and cultures and was suited for children from preschool through early elementary ages. Notable is the inclusion of songs and fingerplays to introduce the next country or culture featured in the program. The program can, of course, be lengthened or shortened depending on local needs.

Día around the World

Begin the program by reading *Whoever You Are*, by Mem Fox. The book includes a simple message: we are all different but all the same under our skin.

Europe—France

Transition

Frère Jacques (*traditional*)	**Brother John**
Frère Jacques, Frère Jacques,	Are you sleeping? Are you sleeping?
Dormez-vous? Dormez-vous?	Brother John, Brother John?
Sonnez les matines.	Morning bells are ringing.
Sonnez les matines.	Morning bells are ringing.
Din, dan, don.	Ding, dang, dong.
Din, dan, don.	Ding, dang, dong.

Prop Story

Use a long snake puppet or stuffed toy to enhance the reading or telling of Tomi Ungerer's *Crictor*, the story of a snake that grows up in a small French town. Start with the snake tightly coiled in a box labeled "Madam Bodot." If desired, have the snake start the story wearing a baby bonnet and show the children a baby paci-fier. Keep the snake in the box and pull out just his head while he is a baby. Use a doll's baby bottle to demonstrate Madam Bodot feeding Crictor. Slowly pull the snake out of the box as he grows until you show the children his entire length. Hold the snake and shape him into letters and numbers as indicated in the story. Other props might include a hat and medal for Crictor, a mask and loot bag for the burglar, and a shawl and reading glasses for Madam Bodot. Of course, also have a book on snakes handy for Madam Bodot to consult when she checks that Crictor is not a poisonous snake.

Book

***Crictor*, by Tomi Ungerer.** When her son sends her a pet snake, Madam Bodot brings him to her class. There he is a very helpful snake, showing the students how to form letters and numbers. But Crictor proves a very resourceful snake when he scares off a burglar.

Africa—Kenya

Transition

"Funga Alafiya, Ashay, Ashay" is a West African call-and-response welcome song. One version of it is on *Jump Up and Sing Binyah's Favorite Songs*, by Gullah Gullah Island (Rhino, 1998):

> **Call:** Funga Alafia
> **Response:** Ashay Ashay

Have a leader sing the call phrase and have the group respond. Use a drum to beat the rhythm between verses. To make this a little more active, the group can make a circle and hold hands as they chant. Move the circle a quarter turn during the drum interlude. Some versions include an English translation for a stanza in between the African words. The English translation can be sung as follows:

> With my thoughts I welcome you
> With my heart I welcome you
> With my words I welcome you
> Funga Alafia Ashay, Ashay

Book

***For You Are a Kenyan Child*, by Kelly Cunnane.** This story shows one day in the life of a Kenyan child through short, poetic phrases. The simple story includes Swahili phrases and cultural details.

Dance Exhibition

Invite a performance group to demonstrate dances from one or more of the countries represented. Alternatively or in addition, let the children learn a simple dance. The dance could be from one of the countries included in the program, such as a Chinese lion dance, or expand the global reach of the program by sharing dance from India, a Polish polka, or the hora from Israel.

Asia—China

Transition

"If You're a Dragon and You Know It": This fingerplay song is sung to the tune of "If You're Happy and You Know It," suiting actions to the words. Make up as many stanzas as you'd like!

> If you're a dragon and you know it, flap your wings.
> > (*Bend arms at the elbows and flap.*)
> If you're a dragon and you know it, flap your wings.
> If you're a dragon and you know it,
> Then your wings will really show it.
> If you're a dragon and you know it, flap your wings.
>
> If you're a dragon and you know it, blow hot fire. (*Purse lips and blow.*)
> If you're a dragon and you know it, blow hot fire.
> If you're a dragon and you know it,
> Then your breath will really show it.
> If you're a dragon and you know it, blow hot fire.

Additional verses:

> Show your claws. (*Stretch fingers out and pretend to claw.*)
> Swish your tail. (*Shake your bottom.*)
> Roar real loud! (*Roar.*)
> Fly away. (*Hold arms out wide and flap them like flying.*)

Book

***Tikki Tikki Tembo,* by Arlene Mosel.** In this classic book, Mosel tells the folktale about the Chinese tradition of giving firstborn sons long, elaborate names and how that tradition came to be changed. The story does not include any Chinese language, but it is a great participation story, as children join in saying, "Tikki tikki tembo-no sa rembo-chari bari ruchi-pip peri pembo."

South America—Peru

Transition

"Row to South America" (song): Make up lyrics as you row your boat down the Amazon River. Alternatively, share a song from Peru; several are provided on Mama Lisa (www.mamalisa.com) and on CDs like *Peru: A Musical Journey,* by various artists (Inside Sounds, 2006).

> Row, row, row your boat
> To South America.

Merrily, merrily, merrily
Floating down the Amazon.

Row, row, row your boat
Down the Amazon
If you see an alligator
Don't forget to scream!

Book

Up and Down the Andes: A Peruvian Festival Tale, **by Laurie Krebs.** In Cusco, the ancient Inca capital, people gather yearly to celebrate Inti Raymi, the New Year. Rhyming text and bright, clear paintings express the rich traditions of Peru.

Australia

Transition

Hop Like Kangaroos: Encourage the children to hop around the room like kangaroos as a transition to the next story, set in Australia.

Story

"The Animal That Couldn't Make Up His Mind" (flannelboard story): This is an Australian Aboriginal creation story. One version is available in *A Twist in the Tail: Animal Stories from around the World,* by Mary Hoffman. Make flannelboard pieces for Yhi, the sun goddess, and the various animals like the kangaroo, lizard, and dingo. For the platypus, use a rat-shaped figure and the various parts the animal wants—a bill, fur, claws, and a flat tail.

Take-Home Craft

Platypus Paper-Bag Puppet

Materials: Paper lunch bags, patterns for platypus parts, crayons, glue sticks, safety scissors

Directions: Enlarge the platypus cutouts on a photocopier and give each child a sheet of platypus parts. Let them color the parts and then cut them out. Place the pieces on the paper lunch bag and glue in place.

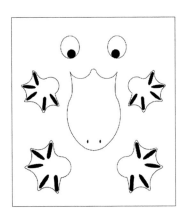

Cutouts for the platypus paper-bag puppet

North America—Mexico

Reader's Theater and Puppetry

Reader's theater offers older children the opportunity to be involved in the program. It's a simple way to share a story without requiring anyone to learn lines as in a play. Many books that can be shared as reader's theater also can be adapted into puppet shows, if preferred. To prepare, print out enough copies of the script for each reader. Highlight each reader's part on the individual copies so that the children know when to read their lines. A puppet-show script for *Isabel and the Hungry Coyote/Isabel y el coyote hambriento*, by Keith Polette, is available as part of the activity sheet provided by the book's publisher (www.deltapublishing .com/worksheets.cfm?OPID=3913). Other resources for Spanish bilingual scripts or Hispanic-themed scripts include *Teatro! Hispanic Plays for Young People*, by Angel Vigil, and *Plays from Hispanic Tales: One-Act, Royalty-Free Dramatizations for Young People, from Hispanic Stories and Folktales*, by Barbara Winther. Although the puppet plays in *One-Person Puppetry Streamlined and Simplified: With 38 Folktale Scripts*, by Yvonne Amar Frey, are not bilingual, it would be a simple matter to translate a few key words in a German tale like "The Smallest Loaf of Bread" to add a multilingual element to the puppet show. One reader's theater script that works very well for El día de los niños/El día de los libros is "The Goat in the Chili Patch," adapted by Rose Zertuche Treviño from a Mexican folktale:

The Goat in the Chili Patch

NARRATOR: Once, a man and a woman lived on a farm, *un rancho*. In their garden, *el jardín*, they grew all sorts of vegetables, but their favorite vegetables of all were the green chili peppers, *los chiles verdes*. One day, a big billy goat, *un cabrito*, broke through the fence and got into their garden and started eating all the ripe *chiles*. The man and the woman ran outside as fast as they could and tried to chase the billy goat out of the garden. They shouted and they pushed and they pulled, but they just couldn't make him leave. So they asked the rooster, *el gallo*, to help them.

MAN: Please, dear friend *gallo*, help us get *el cabrito* out of the chili patch.

GALLO (squawking and pecking): *Cabrito*, get out of the chili patch!

CABRITO: Noooooooooo, you get out.

NARRATOR: *El cabrito* kicked *el gallo* up into the air. And *el cabrito* went right on eating the *chiles*. So the man and woman walked over to the dog, *el perro*, and asked for help.

WOMAN: Please, dear friend *perro*, help us get *el cabrito* out of the chili patch.

PERRO (barking and growling): *Cabrito*, get out of the chili patch!

CABRITO: Noooooooooo, you get out.

NARRATOR: *El cabrito* kicked *el perro* up into the air. And *el cabrito* went right on eating the *chiles*. So the man and woman went over to the bull, *el toro*, and asked for help.

MAN: Please, dear friend *toro*, help us get *el cabrito* out of the chili patch.

NARRATOR: *El toro* snorted and pawed at the ground and gave *el cabrito* his meanest look.

TORO: *Cabrito*, get out of the chili patch!

CABRITO: Nooooooo, you get out.

NARRATOR: *El cabrito* kicked *el toro* up into the air. And *el cabrito* went right on eating the chilis. Just then, a little red ant, *una hormiguita*, came along.

HORMIGUITA: I think I can make *el cabrito* get out of your *chile* patch.

MAN: How can an *hormiguita* do something that *el gallo*, *el perro*, and even *el toro* could not do?

HORMIGUITA: Just watch me.

NARRATOR: *La hormiguita* walked over to *el cabrito*. *El cabrito* didn't even see *la hormiguita* coming. *La hormiguita* walked up *el cabrito*'s back leg. *El cabrito* didn't even feel *la hormiguita* walking. *La hormiguita* walked along *el cabrito*'s back. *El cabrito* still didn't feel *la hormiguita*. *La hormiguita* walked across the soft skin behind *el cabrito*'s ear, and . . . bit him. *El cabrito* jumped up into the air and ran out of the garden as fast as he could. And guess what? He never, ever, ever went near that *chile* patch again.[5]

Closing Song

"Milky Way," by Bill Harley: This song, a modern version of "The Green Grass Grows All Around," reminds us that we all live in the same place. It's on the *Down in the Backpack* album (Round River, 1995), and lyrics are available on Harley's website (www.billharley.com).

Additional Books

***Beyond the Great Mountains: A Visual Poem about China,* by Ed Young.** Through lyrical text and illustrations that include Chinese characters, readers discover the beauty and richness of Chinese culture.

***D Is for Doufu: An Alphabet Book of Chinese Culture,* by Maywan Shen Krach.**

Made in Mexico,
a book about guitars

This beautifully illustrated picture book explains the meanings of twenty-three phrases.

***Dodsworth in Paris,* by Tim Egan.** Dodsworth and his duck visit the French capital and learn a few French words along the way, most of which children can easily understand in the context of the story and illustrations.

***Ernie Dances to the Didgeridoo: For the Children of Gunbalanya,* by Alison Lester.** Ernie heads to the Australian Outback to live. While there, he writes letters to his friends describing Arnhem Land's six seasons and telling about the things his new friends are doing.

***Here Comes the Cat!/Siuda idet kot!* by Frank Asch.** This collaboration between Asch and the Russian author Vladimir Vagin was the first to be published simultaneously in Russia and the United States. The fable tells the story of mice who are afraid of the approaching cat, until they discover that he comes in friendship.

***Honey, Honey—Lion! A Story from Africa,* by Jan Brett.** Based on the legend of an African bird that leads animals to honey, the story is set in the African bush.

***Made in Mexico,* by Peter Laufer and Susan L. Roth.** High in the mountains of Mexico, fine guitars are made in a small town.

***Moon Rope/Un lazo a la luna,* by Lois Ehlert.** In this ancient Peruvian tale, Fox tricks Mole into helping him climb to the moon.

***A Place Where Sunflowers Grow/Sabaku ni saita himawari,* by Amy Lee-Tai.** A young girl adjusts to life in the Topaz Relocation Center during World War II, where she makes a friend and watches the sunflowers grow.

***Stories from the Billabong,* by James Vance Marshall.** Ten Australian Aboriginal folktales explain why things are the way they are. Illustrations reflect the symbols and colors that are important to the Aboriginal people who created them.

Full-Day Programming

El Paso (Texas) Public Library hosts a full-day festival that attracts between twenty thousand and thirty thousand participants. Planning begins in October for a day rich in books, languages, and cultures. An organizing committee works with the city parks department, which is an equal partner in the project. Together, they bring in many community organizations, including many health agencies that also serve children and families. A different theme each year helps focus activities— the 2010 theme, "Rock and Read," highlighted music. Sixty-five booths were set up, representing the various agencies, businesses, and health organizations that participated in the carnival-style celebration. Because of its location on the Mexican border, many of the participants come from Ciudad Juárez, in Mexico. According to Martha A. Toscano, literacy coordinator and head of the organizing committee, the book giveaway is a major part of the cross-border appeal. Although Ciudad Juárez is actually celebrating the Mexican holiday Día del Niño at the same time as El Paso is celebrating El día de los niños/El día de los libros, families love the idea of "book day," which is not celebrated in their hometown. Toscano has found that it is difficult to buy books for children in Juárez. Although books for adults are readily available, few books are published for children and the prices are high.

Budgeting is critical for a full-day program, and you will probably want to have a fund-raising committee. You will also need a lot of volunteers! Other issues to consider include parking, food vendors, and access to bathroom facilities. A full-day festival is a major undertaking and one that requires a great deal of experience and support.

Committees to Consider

Organizing Committee. Sometimes called the executive committee or planning committee, this group is responsible for overseeing the festival. Usually the committee acts as a steering committee, and members serve as liaisons to other committees so

The Big Book Giveaway, sponsored by Target

that the organizing committee knows what is going on and what is still needed.

Book-Giveaway Committee. Research has demonstrated that owning books is a key factor in literacy and reading. Many Día events include a book giveaway. This committee is responsible for selecting and procuring books to give away and for handling the logistics of the distribution at the event. Committee members work closely with the fund-raising committee to secure funds to purchase books and in-kind donations.

Community Outreach Committee. This committee invites community partners to participate in the celebration. It also works to ensure that each participating business or agency knows what is expected, what to do, when to do it, and where to be. A subcommittee might also visit schools to develop partnerships and to encourage students and families to attend events.

Entertainment Committee. Working within the established budget, this committee searches for the various presenters and performers. They invite the performers to participate; negotiate fees and honoraria, if appropriate; and work with the planning committee to establish the schedule for the day's performances. They also work with logistics to ensure that appropriate audiovisual equipment, such as public-address systems, amplifiers, microphones, and other sound equipment are available. This committee may also identify individuals who might serve as emcee.

Fund-Raising Committee. Works with other committees to establish a budget and solicits funds and in-kind donations needed to carry out the event.

Hospitality Committee. Ensures that volunteers and community partners are taken care of during the event. This may include providing bottled water and food, establishing a hospitality room where workers can take breaks, and providing small thank-you gifts or certificates of appreciation.

Logistics Committee. For a large-scale celebration, a logistics committee can ensure that tents are set up, that chairs are rented and in place, and that portable toilets and other necessities are available. Logistics might also help with parking and shuttle buses, if needed, and with trash pickup and other after-event requirements.

Publicity Committee. It's important to get the word out. Some libraries have a communications or public relations department to handle the creation of flyers and bookmarks, sending press releases to the media and working to get media coverage. The publicity committee works to ensure that the library reaches all appropriate venues so that the community knows about the event. Responsibilities may include identifying appropriate venues for promotion, being available for press interviews, and distributing posters and flyers to partner organizations and other locations.

Vendors Committee. If businesses will sell food or other items, you may want a committee to deal with ensuring that the vendors understand the rules and that they comply with local food-handling ordinances.

Volunteers Committee. This committee works to ensure that there is sufficient help for the day. Volunteers will be needed to help with crowd control, to provide directional information, to help with book distribution and other activities, to serve as emcee for the main stage, to pick up trash, and to ensure that everything goes as planned.

Opening Ceremony

Start the daylong program with a celebratory ceremony to kick things off. This provides an opportunity to welcome everyone to the event, to recognize and thank dignitaries and the volunteers and staff, and to set the tone for the day. Use the main stage or focal area for your opening ceremonies.

Main Stage

The main stage will be the focal point of events. Designate an area as the main stage even if it is not actually a platform or formal stage. The area should be large enough to accommodate a good-sized group and should be away from the smaller, quieter booths and activities. Plan performances to fit different periods of time, to allow people to come and go from the area. Also, mix up the type of performance so that you have a rich blend of programming and so that participants don't feel like they missed "all the good stuff." If you have included costumed characters, like Dora the Explorer or the Cat in the Hat, they can introduce storytellers or readers and attract the audience to specific performances.

Many libraries have found that using local performers and children's performance groups is very rewarding. As Tina Birkholz, of the Gail Borden Public Library in Elgin, Illinois, suggests, families come to see their loved ones in action. Local performers also draw in an audience and may be less expensive and willing to give back to the community by donating or discounting their fees. An elementary school may have a folkloric group or a mariachi band. Cultural centers frequently have performance groups that will do authentic dances and play music that is indigenous to their homeland. The Indian cultural center may have dance troupes or Bollywood dancers, or the Chinese cultural center may have a dragon team. For many years, the Miami–Dade County (Florida) Public Library System has partnered with libraries in foreign countries to introduce world-class storytellers, authors, and cultural icons to members of the local community during its annual Art of Storytelling International Festival.

Although the emphasis should be on literacy, keep in mind that literacy comes in many different forms, and books and reading can, and should, be connected to any topic. Ask performers to mention and even show a favorite book that helped them prepare for their act. Perhaps the performer would read a favorite poem related to their talent before the performance.

Provide bookmarks that tie into the program. ALA Graphics (www.alastore .ala.org), Demco (www.demco.com), and other library suppliers offer a wide range of bookmarks and other small book-related giveaways that can support the performances. Many libraries have used the ALA Read software to create products featuring local celebrities as readers. A craft tie-in might ask the children to design their own bookmark to celebrate bilingual literacy. Display the designs and print several of the winners after adding information about the library and El día de los niños/El día de los libros on the reverse side.

Ancillary Activities

Invite local organizations to set up booths or tables for activities. Many libraries require that ancillary activities be provided that link in some way to reading, education, literacy, or learning. Commercial and nonprofit organizations may want to participate but only to distribute information about their services and products. Each booth should provide a free interactive activity for the children and, if possible, have a component that encourages reading or have a reading theme. Even a carnival-style dunking booth can be redesigned so that a literary character is getting dunked! Most libraries also set guidelines about what vendors can sell, often limiting sales to low-cost food. The idea is to keep the festivities as open to all as possible. Potential activity categories include the following:

- art activities
- coloring sheets
- crafts
- face painting
- food creations (healthy treats and recipes)
- games and puzzles
- henna hand painting
- magic tricks
- photographs with costumed literary characters
- puppetry
- safety practice (bike rodeo, fire safety, stranger danger)
- yo-yo exhibition and trials

The Kenton County (Kentucky) Public Library has been working with El día de los niños/El día de los libros since 2004, and its programming has expanded from a small celebration that attracted thirty to forty people to a full day of programming that reaches more than five hundred people, not including ancillary programming in schools and other locations. The library's program consisted primarily of a bilingual storytime with readings of the same book in multiple languages. Using *The Swirling Hijaab*, by Na'ima bint Robert, and *Splash!* by Flora McDonnell, sequential readings were conducted in up to fifteen languages. The multilingual and multicultural program then offered dances from Kuwait, Morocco, and Lebanon; songs from Israel; and salsa-dancing lessons. The program concluded with *cascarones* (confetti eggs) and piñatas.

Farmington (New Mexico) Public Library hosts a long day of celebrations and sets up the parking lot to accommodate vendors and partner organizations. A picture here also shows one of the partner organizations demonstrating how it backs up its vehicles and displays material from the tailgate.

Multiple-Day Programming

Broward County (Florida) Library hosts Children's BookFest each year in recognition of El día de los niños/El día de los libros. The 2010 theme was "One World, Many Stories: The Oceans Link Us Together." Keeping this theme or something similar in mind is a great way to incorporate a number of different cultures into Día activities. Building on past experiences, Broward County Library expanded its programming from a single-day, in-house program to one big program held over

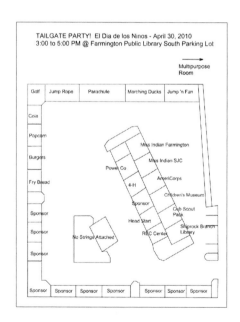

The layout for the Farmington Día tailgate party

A participant shows off a tailgate display at the Farmington party

Resources for Finding Storytellers

National Storytelling Network | www.storynet.org

The storyteller directory provides information about professional storytellers from around the country.

Tejas Storytelling Association | www.tejasstorytelling.com

Although this guild is regional, it serves as a model for other regional guilds, and many of the tellers are nationally known. State associations also frequently have links to local guilds that may be able to help with tellers closer to home.

several days and celebrated at multiple locations around the county. According to librarian Freda Mosquera, this allowed the library to book more prestigious and well-known performers and to use them at multiple events and locations. The library also hired bilingual emcees so that introductions could be made in both English and Spanish. A unique aspect of the programming was a "meet the illustrator" component, which allowed budding artists to learn from award-winning illustrator David Díaz. Not every library can host a big-name illustrator, but most communities have artists who can work with the children.

Multiple-day programming will require similar committees and sharing of responsibilities as outlined in the previous section on full-day programming for Día. Multiple-day events frequently include several locations or venues either spread throughout the community or in a large facility. Events may be held outdoors. A lot of help and coordination are essential for the success of this type of program, as it takes on a festival atmosphere. Be sure to check with local authorities for rules and ordinances, such as the need to have a noise permit for amplified music, that may affect your programming. The example provided here is based on the kickoff activities held on the first evening of Broward County's three-day BookFest. It can be tailored to local opportunities and even be spread out over multiple weekends.

Storytelling under the Stars set the stage for an evening of activities that encouraged working families to participate. Storytelling provides a powerful link to cultures and language. Most cultures have a rich oral heritage that allows elders to pass on stories and lessons to youths. Whether in the evening or during the day, schedule a series of storytellers who will perform for fifteen to thirty minutes each. Look for storytellers in your community or use some of the national databases. Include a mix of tellers from different cultures, and don't shy away from having tellers who tell tales in a language other than English. Part of the performance art frequently includes being able to convey the meaning of the story without words.

Refreshments can be as simple as encouraging families to bring their own. Ask the Friends of the Library or a local vendor to supply popcorn and lemonade, or advertise that food will be available for purchase during the storytelling event and contract with a local restaurant or caterer. Consider offering food from the cultures represented in the community.

Additional Activities

To provide additional opportunities for families to interact with literacy and books, provide activity tables or booths where children and families can create multilingual and multicultural items or participate in specific activities during the storytelling.

Create a Book

One of the easiest ways to share literature in another language is to allow families to create their own books.

Materials: 3-by-5-inch index cards in various colors; hole punch; binder rings; pencils, colored pens, or crayons; stickers (optional); rubber stamps and ink pads (optional)

Directions: Distribute several index cards to each participant. Punch two holes along the top edge of the cards, making sure that they line up nicely. Use the pencils, pens, and crayons to write short stories, poetry, or words in whatever language desired. Use the rubber stamps and stickers to decorate the book and to create a nice cover card. "Bind" by adding two binder rings to create a family book.

There are many other ways to create family books, so check craft books and websites. Alternatively, there are websites like Nellie Edge (www.nellieedge.com/free%20little%20books.htm) that have downloadable tiny books. Download and print a free copy of one of the books (a few titles are available in Spanish, but most are English only). Parents or caregivers can help children by writing out a translation of the story. Enchanted Learning (www.enchantedlearning.com) and other preschool and elementary websites also offer free downloadable books in Spanish, French, German, Chinese, and Italian, but the templates can also serve as models for other languages. Tikatok (www.tikatok.com/library) offers an online workshop for children to create a book and have it "published" in hardback, paperback, or PDF format for inclusion in the library's collection.

Following the kickoff event, use other ideas provided in this book to create multiday programming. Invite local celebrities to be guest readers. Host a "read-in" time each week with a different person reading a book every time. Local celebrities can be almost anyone: politicians, media personalities, university or high school athletes, artists, musicians, educators. Celebrity readers can read a book they enjoyed in childhood or a book from their own culture. Each of these readers will attract his or her own audience, but be sure to ask for their help in publicizing their participation. Enhance the short programs with displays of books and refreshments during a meet-and-greet time. Assist the celebrity reader and expand the program by adding some fun activities, songs, and rhymes. This type of program also works well in schools, where the guest reader can be invited for a general assembly or to read a short book right after lunch.

Books Highlighted

Asch, Frank, and Vladimir Vasilevich Vagin. *Here Comes the Cat!/Sinda idet kot!* New York: Scholastic, 1989. (In English and Russian)

Benjamin, Floella. *Skip across the Ocean: Nursery Rhymes from around the World.* New York: Orchard Books, 1995.

Blia Xiong. *Nine-in-One, Grr! Grr! A Folktale from the Hmong People of Laos.* San Francisco: Children's Book Press, 1989.

Bouchard, David, and Shelley Willier. *The Drum Calls Softly.* Calgary: Red Deer Press, 2008.

Braman, Arlette N. *Kids around the World Play! The Best Fun and Games from Many Lands.* New York: John Wiley and Sons, 2002.

Brett, Jan. *Honey, Honey—Lion! A Story from Africa.* New York: G. P. Putnam's Sons, 2005.

Chorao, Kay. *Rhymes round the World.* New York: Dutton Children's Books, 2009.

Cunnane, Kelly. *For You Are a Kenyan Child.* New York: Atheneum Books for Young Readers, 2006.

Diamant-Cohen, Betsy. *Early Literacy Programming en español: Mother Goose on the Loose Programs for Bilingual Learners.* New York: Neal-Schuman Publishers, 2010.

Dunn, Opal. *Un deux trois: First French Rhymes.* London: Frances Lincoln Children's, 2006.

Egan, Tim. *Dodsworth in Paris.* Boston: Houghton Mifflin, 2008.

Ehlert, Lois. *Moon Rope: A Peruvian Folktale/Un lazo a la luna: Una leyenda peruana.* San Diego, CA: Harcourt Brace Jovanovich, 1992.

Fox, Mem. *Whoever You Are.* San Diego, CA: Harcourt Brace, 1997.

Frey, Yvonne Amar. *One-Person Puppetry Streamlined and Simplified: With 38 Folktale Scripts.* Chicago: American Library Association, 2005.

Hoffman, Mary, and Jan Ormerod. *A Twist in the Tail: Animal Stories from around the World.* New York: Henry Holt, 1998.

Isadora, Rachel. *Say Hello!* New York: G. P. Putnam's Sons, 2010.

Krach, Maywan Shen. *D Is for Doufu: An Alphabet Book of Chinese Culture.* Arcadia, CA: Shen's Books, 1997.

Krebs, Laurie. *Up and Down the Andes: A Peruvian Festival Tale.* Cambridge, MA: Barefoot Books, 2008.

Laínez, René Colato. *Playing lotería / El juego de la lotería.* Flagstaff, AZ: Luna Rising, a Bilingual Imprint of Rising Moon, 2005.

Lankford, Mary D. *Dominoes around the World.* New York: Morrow Junior Books, 1998.

———. *Hopscotch around the World.* New York: Morrow Junior Books, 1992.

———. *Jacks around the World.* New York: Morrow Junior Books, 1996.

Laufer, Peter, and Susan L. Roth. *Made in Mexico.* Washington, DC: National Geographic Society, 2000.

Law, Diane. *Come Out and Play: Count around the World in Five Languages.* Zurich, Switzerland: NordSud Verlag, 2006.

Lee-Tai, Amy. *A Place Where Sunflowers Grow / Sabaku ni saita himawari.* San Francisco, CA: Children's Book Press, 2006.

Lester, Alison. *Ernie Dances to the Didgeridoo: For the Children of Gunbalanya.* Boston: Houghton Mifflin, 2000.

Lin, Grace. *The Ugly Vegetables.* Watertown, MA: Charlesbridge, 1999.

Louis, Catherine, Mary Chris Bradley, and Bo Shi. *My Little Book of Chinese Words.* New York: NorthSouth Books, 2008.

Marshall, James Vance. *Stories from the Billabong.* London: Frances Lincoln Children's, 2008.

McDonnell, Flora. *Splash!* Cambridge, MA: Candlewick Press, 1999.

McQuinn, Anna. *Lola at the Library.* Watertown, MA: Charlesbridge, 2006.

———. *Lulu Loves the Library.* Berkshire, UK: Alanna Books, 2006.

Mora, Pat. *Join Hands! The Ways We Celebrate Life.* Watertown, MA: Charlesbridge, 2008.

Morgenstern, Christian. *Lullabies, Lyrics and Gallows Songs.* New York: NorthSouth Books, 1995.

Mosel, Arlene. *Tikki Tikki Tembo.* New York: Holt, Rinehart, and Winston, 1968.

Pascale, Louise M. *Children's Songs from Afghanistan/Qu qu qu barg-e-chinaar.* Washington, DC: National Geographic, 2008.

Polette, Keith. *Isabel and the Hungry Coyote / Isabel y el coyote hambriento.* McHenry, IL: Raven Tree Press, 2004. (Originally published in 1970)

Robert, Na'ima bint. *The Swirling Hijaab.* London: Mantra, 2002.

Ryll, Debra. *Tūtū Nēnē: The Hawaiian Mother Goose Rhymes.* Aiea, HI: Island Heritage, 1997.

Schiller, Pamela Byrne, Rafael Lara-Alecio, and Beverly J. Irby. *The Bilingual Book of Rhymes, Songs, Stories, and Fingerplays / El libro bilingüe de rimas, canciones, cuentos y juegos.* Beltsville, MD: Gryphon House, 2004.

Treviño, Rose Zertuche. *Read Me a Rhyme in Spanish and English / Léame una rima en español e inglés.* Chicago: American Library Association, 2009.

Ungerer, Tomi. *Crictor.* New York: Harper, 1958.

Vigil, Angel. *Teatro! Hispanic Plays for Young People.* Englewood, CO: Teacher Ideas

Press, 1996.

Waddell, Martin. *Farmer Duck.* Cambridge, MA: Candlewick Press, 1992.

Winther, Barbara. *Plays from Hispanic Tales: One-Act, Royalty-Free Dramatizations for Young People, from Hispanic Stories and Folktales.* Boston: Plays Inc., 1998.

Wright, Danielle. *My Village: Rhymes from around the World.* London: Frances Lincoln Children's, 2010.

Wu, Faye-Lynn. *Chinese and English Nursery Rhymes: Share and Sing in Two Languages.* North Clarendon, VT: Tuttle, 2010.

Wyndham, Robert. *Chinese Mother Goose Rhymes.* New York: Philomel Books, 1989.

Yolen, Jane. *Sleep Rhymes around the World.* Honesdale, PA: Wordsong/Boyds Mills Press, 1994.

———. *Street Rhymes around the World.* Honesdale, PA: Boyds Mills Press, 2005.

Young, Ed. *Beyond the Great Mountains: A Visual Poem about China.* San Francisco: Chronicle Books, 2005.

Notes

1. Lella Gandini and Simonetta Sambrotta, "Italian Nursery Rhymes: A Rich, Varied, and Well-Used Landscape," *Lion and the Unicorn* 26 (April 2002): 203.
2. Translation by Rossella Pivanti; used with permission.
3. Translation by Monica Khosla; used with permission.
4. Translation by Alexandra Corona; used with permission.
5. Adapted by Rose Treviño. Reprinted from *Color Your World . . . Read! 2004 Texas Reading Club Manual,* by Jeanette Larson and Rose Zertuche Treviño. Used with permission.

6
Programming— Celebrating Día in Schools

Schools can include celebrations of multiple literacies in their special and routine activities. Although any of the ideas included in this book can be tailored for the school environment, there are other considerations as well. As you begin to plan your celebration, be sure to look at the basics of program planning discussed in chapter 3. The suggestions there will help you plan the program effectively and efficiently.

Many school libraries cannot support a major event or series of events right around April 30 because of end-of-year testing. It is acceptable to set your own dates for Día programming. Host a celebration near that date that works for your students, families, and faculty. Partner with the parent-teacher organization to include parents and other family members in the festivities. Download and print copies of the El día de los niños/El día de los libros brochure from the Association for Library Service to Children (www.ala.org/ala/mgrps/divs/alsc/initiatives/diadelosninos/diaresources/diaresources.cfm) for distribution to parents. Host a shared reading of *Book Fiesta! Celebrate Children's Day/Book Day / Celebremos El día de los niños/El día de los libros*, by Pat Mora. This book is a great way to introduce the concepts of Día. An option is to have a different book, based on age appropriateness, read to each grade level. Use the bibliographies provided in this book to find titles appropriate for the cultures being celebrated. Ask the school cafeteria to serve foods from different cultures for lunch, with signs indicating what the food is in the native language.

Many school librarians find themselves stretched among several schools, each vying for limited time. Karen Meno, the elementary school library coordinator for the Forney Independent School District in Texas, plans to start programming for

El día de los niños/El día de los libros but works with four schools. She will start small, working with one school that has a high bilingual student population. It's also a good idea to involve the parent-teacher organization. Meno plans to use the local parent-teacher organization to host a book exchange, whereby families can exchange books during a special evening for El día de los niños/El día de los libros. This can become the basis for events at other schools and provide the foundation for more programming.

School librarians and teachers may feel that they cannot add anything more to their already-packed day and therefore be reluctant to add El día de los niños/El día de los libros programming. Alma Ramos-McDermott, the school librarian at Pollard Middle School in Needham, Massachusetts, points out that you can add new things if you are willing to give up on something else or tweak what you are doing to take on a new focus. She says that Día activities can be viewed as teachable moments. Although her school is predominantly an Anglo, English-speaking population, she recognizes that bilingual literacy introduces her students to literature they would not normally be exposed to and that reading books in Spanish helps them to make connections between their own language and new languages. She also views Día activities as a means to provide bridges between cultures. Ramos-McDermott points to April as School Library Media Month and suggests that bilingual programming and books be incorporated into already planned activities. The 2010 theme "Communities Thrive @ your library" was a perfect fit for spotlighting non-English-speaking and non-European cultures. Check the American Association of School Librarians website (www.ala.org/ala/mgrps/divs/aasl/aaslissues/slm/schoollibrary.cfm) for future themes and activity ideas. Working in a middle school, Ramos-McDermott also tailors the concept of El día de los niños/El día de los libros to her students by referring to the celebration as El día de los jóvenes/El día de los libros to reflect "youths" rather than "children" as the audience. In fact, her school celebrates for a week, Semana de los jóvenes/Semana de los libros, and she works with different teachers and students each day.

A child participates in Spanish-language Día activities

Finding funds for programming and materials can be challenging. If school policy permits, look to organizations like DonorsChoose (www.donorschoose.org) for help. This online charity matches donors with educational groups that need funds, and many donors support efforts toward bilingual literacy. First Book (www.firstbook .org) and local public television stations also work with schools to provide books for distribution to children and can often provide books in Spanish or bilingual books.

Because schools have a built-in audience, it is easy to add bilingual books to library storytimes and book sharing. The librarian can also recommend bilingual and multicultural titles for classroom use. Teachers often stick with tried-and-true books and miss out on the many wonderful new titles that are available. Offer copies of titles listed in resources like the bibliography provided in the Association for Library Service to Children's Día tool kit (www.ala.org/ala/mgrps/divs/alsc/initiatives/diadelosninos/diaresources/Random%20House%20Tool%20Kit%20download.pdf) or the El día de los niños/El día de los libros brochure (www.ala.org/ala/mgrps/divs/alsc/initiatives/diadelosninos/diacelebrations/dia09brodnld.pdf). You can copy these bibliographies for distribution, or use the lists to collect books for a display in the library. Also, REFORMA provides book lists in the Children's and Young Adult Services section of its website (www.reforma.org/CYASC.htm).

Another idea is to offer a short choral reading or reader's-theater activity during lunch or as an assembly. Aaron Shepard provides scripts based on his books (www.aaronshep.com). Many reflect stories from different cultures, some of which have even been translated into traditional Chinese. Grace Lin (www.gracelin.com) provides a script for a theatrical adaptation of *The Ugly Vegetables* that elementary school children could perform for parents and classmates.

Work with the English-language-learner (ELL) or bilingual education coordinator. He or she not only will have programming ideas and suggestions for ways to tie bilingual learning into your activities but also may be able to offer resources and links to parent and community volunteers who speak and read other languages. Spring Mills Middle School, in Martinsburg, West Virginia, featured the Spanish teacher reading a book over the public-address system for its Día celebration. Ramos-McDermott works with the Spanish-language classes at her middle school to provide bilingual book talks during the days leading up to Día. In addition to translations of middle-grade books, she uses higher-level picture books, like *César Chávez: The Struggle for Justice/César Chávez: La lucha por la justicia*, by Richard Griswold del Castillo, or *The Bossy Gallito/El gallo de bodas: A Traditional Cuban Folktale*, retold by Lucía M. González. Students learning a new language are also encouraged to write original poetry in that language or to partner with another student to read a book jointly.

Adding to the curriculum that is already in place means that you can add bilingual literacy without much additional work. Former library media specialist Adrienne Ehlert Bashista recommends short bursts of Día activities during regular classroom activities. She presented tandem readings with the Spanish teacher, invited bilingual authors and storytellers for special presentations, and integrated culture into the activities to make them more meaningful and to provide connections for the students. Following a presentation by author Caroline McAlister and a reading of her book *Holy Mole! A Folktale from Mexico*, students enjoyed a *mole* tasting, comparing recipes to find the one they liked best. Check out the lesson plans that the book's publisher, August House (www.augusthouse.com), offers for additional curriculum ideas for the book. In addition to working with language arts and social studies lessons, a fun way to use a story like *Holy Mole!* is to consider other meanings of the word *mole*. October 23 is a national celebration of Mole Day, but in this case the mole is a unit of measurement in chemistry. Of course, a mole is also a burrowing animal or a small growth on the skin or a spy in an organization. One of the delightful aspects of language is that words that look the same can have very different pronunciations and meanings!

Many language arts teachers would welcome a project that encourages students to write their own bilingual book. Use a resource like the National Writing Project's *Our Book by Us!/Nuestro libro ¡hecho por nosotros!* (www.nwp.org/cs/public/print/resource/2567) for a quick and easy project. Targeted to younger children, each minibook has a story with activity pages that invite the students to add details about their own life experiences.

Feature bilingual dictionaries so that children can learn a few words in another language. Books like *Hippocrene Children's Illustrated Chinese (Mandarin) Dictionary: English-Chinese/Chinese-English* and *Milet Mini Picture Dictionary: English-Farsi*, by Sedat Turhan and Sally Hagin, allow students to quickly pick up a familiar word in another language in a short period of time. Children can also be encouraged to create their own picture dictionary using templates like those from Enchanted Learning (www.enchantedlearning.com/books/mini/).

Host a folktale festival. Use folktales and fairy tales to show cross-cultural ideas and incorporate both multilingualism and multiculturalism into lessons. There are versions of the Cinderella story in almost every culture, so a full day of programming could be centered around a single story. *Book Links* published "Multicultural Cinderella Stories," by Mary Northrup (available in electronic format at www.ala.org/ala/aboutala/offices/publishing/booklinks/resources/multicultural.cfm). Northrup's article includes a nice list of picture books and novels featuring Cinderella in a variety of cultures. *Cinderella: The Oryx Multicultural Folktale Series*, by Judy Sierra, provides twenty-four translations of authentic text from around the globe and includes cultural background information to set the stories in context. Invite community members to dress in traditional costumes from some of the cultures represented in the stories. Alternatively, let the students make paper dolls with traditional clothes from the countries and cultures about which they are hearing stories. Multicultural Kids (www.multiculturalkids.com/Costumes/) and other online retailers sell costumes, doll kits, and puppets that reflect other cultures.

Reader's theater can be a way to involve the community in bilingual literacy. Aaron Shepard's website (www.aaronshep.com/rt/RTE03_Chinese.html) provides a free translated script in Chinese for his retelling of *Savitri: A Tale of Ancient India*. Several other stories are similarly available. Ask parents who read and speak Chinese to perform the story. A reader's-theater script for *Jouanah: A Hmong Cinderella*, by Jewell Reinhart Coburn, is available from the publisher, Shen's Books (www.shens.com) in the teacher guide provided for the book. A great thing about reader's theater is that little or no practice is required!

Host a read-in. Some organizations, like the International Reading Association and the Black Caucus of the National Council of Teachers of English, sponsor read-ins. These include Hispanic American Read-in Chain (in September) and

African American Read-in Chain (in February), but schools can highlight any culture and books about that culture by hosting a read-in. Select books and make them available for public readings. This might happen during lunch by inviting teachers and parents to read aloud throughout the lunch period or by having each class read a book at the same time on a specific day. The idea is to create a "chain" of readers sharing bookjoy!

In Woodburn, Oregon, 950 family members and friends gathered for a celebration that was customized to the community's ethnic configuration. Although the majority of ethnic groups in Woodburn are Anglo and Hispanic, a growing Russian community is being integrated into El día de los niños/El día de los libros programming. Collaborators included school staff but also local service groups like Rotary clubs, the public library, and many businesses, which resulted in the creation of community spirit. Hope Crandall, a librarian at Washington Elementary School in Woodburn, believes that the success of multilingual programming lies in tying it to the school's mandate for parent involvement and family literacy. In a 2009 article in *OLA Quarterly*, Crandall, Parra, and Chamberlain offer a number of suggestions for literacy-based activities, including asking family members to write or illustrate favorite riddles and proverbs, making a book-based character available in costume for family photos, and playing a Wheel of Fortune–type game using book-related puzzles.[1]

The National Education Association supports literacy events like El día de los niños/El día de los libros and provides a diversity calendar online (www.nea .org/grants/1360.htm). Use the calendar or *Chase's Calendar of Events 2011* to find important cultural holidays or special days for your community. Let teachers and staff know ahead of time about books related to that holiday or culture that can be shared in the classroom. Resources like the bibliographies provided in other sections of this book, as well as titles like *Windows on the World*, by Rosanne Blass; *Across Cultures: A Guide to Multicultural Literature for Children*, by Kathy East and Rebecca L. Thomas; and *Understanding Diversity through Novels and Picture Books*, by Liz Knowles and Martha Smith, can provide help in locating titles that represent many different cultures and communities.

Of course, schools are also great partners for public libraries that are planning El día de los niños/El día de los libros celebrations. Austin (Texas) Public Library often uses the school and public library joint facility to host their community's celebration. Ask the public library how your school can support El día de los niños/ El día de los libros programming and how you can work together to bring bilingual programming to students.

Potential Celebrations

February 21: International Mother Language Day

Proclaimed by the United Nations, this day recognizes that "Languages are the most powerful instruments of preserving and developing our tangible and intangible heritage." *Can You Greet the Whole Wide World? Twelve Common Phrases in Twelve Different Languages*, by Lezlie Evans, is a good book to use to start a campaign to learn to greet students and teachers in a new language each morning. Post phrases on poster board around the school. There are also a few polyglot books, providing the text in multiple languages in the same book, that could be shared. Try *Who Hides in the Park*, by Warabé Aska, which features a story in English, French, Japanese, and Chinese.

March 3: World Read-Aloud Day

A new celebration that began in 2010, World Read-Aloud Day is a campaign of LitWorld. It offers a great opportunity to read aloud from longer books that reflect the world's cultures. Resources like *Reid's Read-Alouds: Selections for Children and Teens*, by Rob Reid, provide suggestions for selections from popular books. Poetry, such as selections from *A Suitcase of Seaweed, and Other Poems*, by Janet S. Wong, or *Nineteen Varieties of Gazelle: Poems of the Middle East*, by Naomi Shihab Nye, is also great for oral sharing and offers insights into the writer's culture.

September 8: International Literacy Day

This UNESCO-sponsored event (www.unesco.org/en/literacy/advocacy/international -literacy-day/) serves to remind "the international community of the status of literacy and adult learning globally." Buckner Elementary School in Pharr, Texas, celebrated by inviting parents to read to fifth-grade students. Enhance the concepts of global literacy by reading bilingual books. The International Reading Association offers a tool kit with ideas for promoting international literacy. Check out the ideas at Reading.org (www.reading.org/Libraries/Association_documents/2010_IDEA_ STARTERS.pdf)—one involves sharing international newspapers. Use the Internet to find examples of online newspapers and share front-page news with students. Many newspapers, like Austria's *Der Standard* (http://epaper.derstandarddigital.at/) share digital images of the news. Locate newspapers through Yahoo!'s directory (http:// dir.yahoo.com/News_and_Media/Newspapers/By_Region/Countries/).

September 17: Citizenship Day

Use this day to focus on new immigrants and the wonderful diversity of our country. Read *Hannah Is My Name: A Young Immigrant's Story*, by Belle Yang, or *My Shoes and I*, by René Colato Laínez.

October 6: German American Day

A 1983 proclamation recognized this day when the first German families arrived in America in 1683. Read a fairy tale, like "Hansel and Gretel" or "The Bremen Town Musicians" that came to us from Germany. Rachel Isadora has retold and published *Hansel and Gretel* in an African setting for a multicultural experience, and Doris Orgel's *The Bremen Town Musicians, and Other Animal Tales from Grimm* sticks to the more traditional story told in her own translation. Many of these traditional European folktales are also readily available in translations to other languages. *Count Your Way through Germany,* by James Haskins, is also a good way to introduce simple German words to children.

Third Monday in October: Multicultural Diversity Day

The National Education Association has encouraged teachers to celebrate diversity on this day for a decade and the NEA website offers a diversity tool kit to help educators improve their cultural competencies. Use a book like *What a Wonderful World,* by George David Weiss and Bob Thiele, to share the wonder of our culturally rich world.

Books Highlighted

Aska, Warabé. *Who Hides in the Park.* Toronto: Tundra, 1992.

Blass, Rosanne J. *Windows on the World: International Books for Elementary and Middle Grade Readers.* Santa Barbara, CA: Library Unlimited/ABC-CLIO, 2010.

Chase's Calendar of Events 2011. New York: McGraw-Hill, 2010.

Coburn, Jewell Reinhart. Illus. by Tzexa Cherta Lee. *Jouanah: A Hmong Cinderella.* Walnut Creek, CA: Shen's Books, 1996.

Colato Laínez, René. *My Shoes and I.* Honesdale, PA: Boyds Mills Press, 2010.

East, Kathy, and Rebecca L. Thomas. *Across Cultures: A Guide to Multicultural Literature for Children.* Westport, CT: Libraries Unlimited, 2007.

Evans, Lezlie. *Can You Greet the Whole Wide World? Twelve Common Phrases in Twelve Different Languages.* Boston: Houghton Mifflin, 2006.

González, Lucía M. *The Bossy Gallito / El gallo de bodas: A Traditional Cuban Folktale.* New York: Scholastic, 1994.

Griswold del Castillo, Richard. *César Chávez: The Struggle for Justice/César Chávez: La lucha por la justicia.* Hispanic Civil Rights Series. Houston, TX: Piñata Books, 2002.

Haskins, James. *Count Your Way through Germany.* Minneapolis, MN: Carolrhoda Books, 1990.

Hippocrene Children's Illustrated Chinese (Mandarin) Dictionary: English-Chinese, Chinese-English. New York: Hippocrene Books, 2001.

Isadora, Rachel. *Hansel and Gretel.* New York: G. P. Putnam's Sons, 2009.

Knowles, Elizabeth, and Martha Smith. *Understanding Diversity through Novels and Picture Books.* Westport, CT: Libraries Unlimited, 2007.

Lin, Grace. *The Ugly Vegetables.* Watertown, MA: Charlesbridge, 1999.

McAlister, Caroline. *Holy Mole! A Folktale from Mexico*. Little Rock, AR: August House LittleFolk, 2007.

Mora, Pat. *Book Fiesta! Celebrate Children's Day/Book Day/Celebremos El día de los niños/El día de los libros*. New York: HarperCollins, 2009.

Nye, Naomi Shihab. *Nineteen Varieties of Gazelle: Poems of the Middle East*. New York: Greenwillow Books, 2002.

Orgel, Doris. *The Bremen Town Musicians, and Other Animal Tales from Grimm*. Brookfield, CT: Roaring Brook Press, 2004.

Reid, Rob. *Reid's Read-Alouds: Selections for Children and Teens*. Chicago: American Library Association, 2009.

Shepard, Aaron. *Savitri: A Tale of Ancient India*. Morton Grove, IL: Albert Whitman, 1992.

Sierra, Judy. *Cinderella: The Oryx Multicultural Folktale Series*. Santa Barbara, CA: Oryx Press, 1992.

Turhan, Sedat, and Sally Hagin. *Milet Mini Picture Dictionary: English-Farsi*. London: Milet, 2009.

Weiss, George David, and Bob Thiele. Illus. by Ashley Bryan. *What a Wonderful World*. New York: Atheneum Books for Young Readers, 1995.

Wong, Janet S. *A Suitcase of Seaweed, and Other Poems*. New York: Margaret K. McElderry Books, 1996.

Yang, Belle. *Hannah Is My Name: A Young Immigrant's Story*. Cambridge, MA: Candlewick Press, 2004.

Note

1. Hope Crandall, Mary Parra, and Deeda Chamberlain, "Community Collaborates for a Día Celebration," *OLA Quarterly* 5 (Winter 2009): 25–27.

Best Practices

E ach community has different opportunities and challenges in programming Día activities. Regardless of whether your celebration is big or small, half a day or ongoing throughout a month, the following successful programs can offer inspiration and ideas. Be sure to check regularly on the Association for Library Service to Children's Día celebrations database (www.ala.org/ala/mgrps/divs/alsc/initiatives/diadelosninos/diacelebrations/diacelebrations.cfm) for the latest updates on how libraries are celebrating El día de los niños/El día de los libros.

The **Albuquerque/Bernalillo County Library System** in New Mexico celebrates Día for two weeks in April. The 2010 events featured presenters from a range of cultures and backgrounds. A key partner for 2010 was the University of New Mexico's Maxwell Museum of Anthropology, which presented programs on weaving and musical instruments from around the world. A storyteller from Alaska shared indigenous stories from Alaskan and Inuit communities, but one of the major components of the program, according to librarian Riann Powell, was "the partnership that our library system has developed with local entertainers and educators; we have built relationships with many of these people and organizations that have sustained beyond an annual program." Following large-scale kickoff events at regional libraries, programs were held at all locations throughout the system. Children received a free book and were able to participate in activities that allowed them to learn stories and poems.

El Paso (Texas) Public Library hosts one of the largest Día celebrations in the country. In 2010, the library gave away ten thousand books. The theme was "Rock and Read," and Dora the Explorer was a guest at the events.

Farmington (New Mexico) Public Library sponsors the Día Tailgate Party. Attendees are encouraged to bring a gift-wrapped book to exchange in a musical-chairs type of game so that each child receives a new-to-them book. In keeping with the theme, books shared featured food. The Día Tailgate Party also served as a kickoff for the summer-reading program, allowing the library staff to reach a lot of parents and encourage continued reading.

Multnomah County (Oregon) Library has hosted a number of very successful Día programs, and it won the 2002 Mora Award for its work. Each year the library uses a different theme for the celebration. For example, the 2010 theme was "Spanish-Speaking Countries." The theme is manifested in activities with local schools and activities for families. For example, a middle school created a large map of the Spanish-speaking countries. Patrons then marked the map with stickers to show the country where their family originated. Families also made informational posters about their homelands and answered trivia questions about the countries. Experience has encouraged the library to reduce the number of performers and focus on adding more literacy activities. A questionnaire-style scavenger hunt encouraged parents to walk around the event seeking answers. During the storytime, as well as when explaining other activities, staff incorporated a few early literacy tips and ideas to help families understand the benefits of early literacy for their children. The program was organized into four areas, marked by large, laminated crayon signs for print awareness, phonological awareness, print motivation, and narrative skills. Library staff and community partners worked each area. As participants went to each station and participated in that activity, a raffle card was stamped for them.

San Francisco Public Library began celebrating Día in 1999, and its festivities have grown dramatically every year. It is the goal of the steering committee to have Día be "an integral part of San Francisco's early childhood and educational landscape,"[1] and the celebration is now part of the library's annual calendar of programs. The culminating events are held outdoors in a park in the Mission District—the district with the highest concentration of Spanish speakers. The event is a collaborative effort, with a steering committee comprising representatives from many community organizations, including the northern California chapter of REFORMA, Bibliotecas para la Gente, and the publisher Children's Book Press. Each year the group looks for new ways to increase community and awareness of the importance of reading "in whatever language . . . is their own." Notable are SFPL's fund-raising efforts, which for 2009 included a silent auction and a tenth-anniversary reception.

San Mateo County (California) Library is a relative newcomer to Día programming, having started its initiative in 2007. By the third year, more than two thousand children and families were attending events at twelve branch libraries along a hundred-mile stretch between San Francisco and San Jose. A key element to San Mateo's programming is the Spanish Services Committee, which comprises bilingual librarians from various branches. Each year the group has pushed itself to find even more partners and collaborators. To that end, it is also encouraging neighboring library systems to join in the collaboration to further expand the reach to more families in northern California.

Smith Public Library in Wylie, Texas, has a tradition of featuring dance during its Día festivities. For several years, the Ballet Folklórico has featured dances from different regions of Mexico, but this tradition could easily be expanded to feature dances from other cultures and countries. Following the demonstration dances, the audience is invited to learn the dance steps.

Topeka and Shawnee County (Kansas) Public Library hosts a fiesta to celebrate Día. In 2009, the fiesta was based on the concept of Carnavalito and featured traditional dances from Bolivia. A local class of English-speaking Spanish learners was invited to present a reader's-theater adaptation of a story in Spanish. A YouTube video showing the reader's-theater presentation can be viewed on the library's website (www.tscpl.org/kids/comments/videos_of_el_dia).

Maricopa County Library District, in Phoenix, Arizona, presented an adaptation of Pat Mora's book *Tomás and the Library Lady* in partnership with the Maricopa Partnership for Arts and Culture.

Safford City–Graham County Library, in Safford, Arizona, hosted a music festival with a performer who performed songs from various countries and cultures in a variety of languages. The festivities also included children making their own books using plastic sandwich bags as pages and other multicultural crafts.

McCall (Idaho) Public Library focuses on reaching non-English-speaking families and partners with the local hospital auxiliary thrift shop. The store provides a free used book for every child attending and "coupons'" for other family members to use for purchases. The participants plant spring flowers at the thrift shop as a community show of appreciation.

Pueblo West Library, in Pueblo, Colorado, held a multilingual storytime with volunteers sharing stories in German, Swahili, Punjabi, Chinese, and Spanish. After the storytime, children created crafts from the represented countries.

Note

1. San Francisco Public Library, application for the 2009 Estela and Raúl Mora Award, August 31, 2009.

Resources

There are many resources available to help libraries plan their El día de los niños/ El día de los libros celebrations, programs, and activities. As Día continues to grow, even more resources will become available. Keep in mind that resources are constantly changing; books go out of print and websites change. The URLs for websites were accurate at the time of printing but may change at any time. If the URL does not produce the expected web page, try searching with the title and description. Also, many of these resources offer links to newly created or compiled resources and continue to add new information and updates, so check them regularly.

Recommended Book Lists and Awards

American Indian Youth
Literature Award | *www.ailanet.org/activities/youthlitaward.htm*
A young award, first granted in 2006, the American Indian Youth Literature Award was created to identify and honor the very best writing and illustrations by and about American Indians. Awards are given in three categories: picture book, middle school, and young adult. Books should reflect the values and worldview of American Indian cultures.

Américas Award for Children's
and Young Adult Literature | *www4.uwm.edu/clacs/aa/*
The Américas Award is given in recognition of works of fiction, poetry, folklore, or nonfiction published in English or Spanish that "authentically and engagingly

portray Latin America, the Caribbean, or Latinos in the United States." The award is sponsored by the national Consortium of Latin American Studies Programs at the University of Wisconsin–Milwaukee. Lists of winning titles are provided back to the inception of the award in 1993.

Asian/Pacific American
Librarians Awards | *www.apalaweb.org/awards/literature-awards/*
Every other year, members of the Asian/Pacific American Librarians Association select outstanding titles in picture-book and text categories.

Batchelder Award | *www.ala.org/ala/mgrps/divs/alsc/awardsgrants/bookmedia/ batchelderaward/*
Unlike many awards that are given to the author or illustrator of a book, the Batchelder Award is a citation awarded to an American publisher. It recognizes a children's book originally published in a language other than English in a country other than the United States and subsequently translated into English and published in the United States. Although many of the books are intended for older readers, each title on the list of current and past winners is a book that furthers efforts "to eliminate barriers to understanding between people of different cultures, races, nations, and languages."

Hans Christian Andersen Awards | *www.ibby.org/index.php?id=273*
The Hans Christian Andersen Award, sponsored by the International Board on Books for Young People (IBBY), is the highest international recognition given to an author and an illustrator of children's books. Each of the national sections in IBBY can nominate candidates. The bibliography of winners serves as a good start on a core collection of books from other countries.

Pura Belpré Medal | *www.ala.org/ala/mgrps/divs/alsc/awardsgrants/bookmedia/ belpremedal/*
Named for the first Latina librarian at New York Public Library, this award recognizes an author and an illustrator for an outstanding work of literature for children and young people that "best portrays, affirms, and celebrates the Latino cultural experience." In addition to the medal winners, honor books are named. The award began in 1996 and until 2008 was presented every other year. It is now an annual award, and current and past winners and honor books are listed on the website.

Sydney Taylor Book Award | *www.jewishlibraries.org/ajlweb/awards/stba/*
Presented by the Association of Jewish Libraries, this annual award is presented to outstanding books for children and teens that authentically portray the Jewish experience.

Tomás Rivera Mexican American

Children's Book Award | *www.education.txstate.edu/departments/Tomas-Rivera-Book -Award-Project-Link.html*
Established in 1995 by the Texas State University College of Education, the Tomás Rivera Award honors authors and illustrators who create literature that depicts the Mexican American experience.

USBBY Outstanding International

Books List | *www.usbby.org/outstanding_international_books_list.htm*
The U.S. Board on Books for Young People annually selects outstanding books that originated or were first published in a country other than the United States. The website includes downloadable resources like bookmarks and exhibit aids.

Publishers

Arte Público Press | *www.artepublicopress.com*
Arte Público is the nation's largest publisher of literature by U.S. Hispanic authors. Its Piñata Books imprint includes children's literature that "authentically and realistically portrays themes, characters, and customs unique to U.S. Hispanic culture," and many titles are bilingual or translated.

August House | *www.augusthouse.com*
Best known for publishing collections of folktales, August House also publishes picture books and audiobooks representing the world's cultures.

Barefoot Books | *www.barefootbooks.com*
A small publishing company, Barefoot Books seeks to publish timeless stories for a global community. Several titles are published in multiple translations, which results in interesting mixtures such as *We All Went on Safari*, a Swahili counting book available in Spanish.

Capstone Books | *www.capstonepub.com*
This publisher produces a number of books in Spanish, including a lot of nonfiction.

Centro de Información y Desarrollo de la Comunicación y Literatura Infantiles (CIDCLI) | *http://cidcli.com.mx*
CIDCLI publishes "high quality literary works written and illustrated by well-known Spanish-speaking authors and outstanding artists from around the world."

Charlesbridge Publishing | *www.charlesbridge.com*
Although Charlesbridge is a publisher of a broad range of high-quality children's books, it features a notable number of bilingual books, including several that "help young readers expand their appreciation of the multicultural world in which they live."

Children's Book Press | *www.childrensbookpress.org*
A nonprofit publisher, Children's Book Press focuses its publishing on "first voice literature for children by and about people from the Latino, African American, Asian/Pacific Islander, and Native American communities." Many of its books feature authentic storytelling from cultures that are typically underrepresented or misrepresented in mainstream publishing.

Chronicle Books | *www.chroniclebooks.com*
Chronicle Books publishes a wide variety of books, many with multicultural themes, and publishes Spanish-language and bilingual translations of many popular fairy tales, science books by Seymour Simon, and more.

Cinco Puntos Press | *www.cincopuntos.com*
A small, independent publishing company in El Paso, Texas, Cinco Puntos Press publishes a fair amount of regional material, including books based in Native American cultures. Many of its books about Hispanic cultures are bilingual or available in translation.

Cooper Square Publishing | *www.coopersquarepublishing.com*
Cooper Square includes imprints for several lines of children's books that feature Southwest and Spanish-speaking cultures. Luna Rising is the bilingual imprint, and books from Rising Moon focus on the southwestern United States.

Cultural Connections | *www.culture-connect.org*
Established by a consortium of educators, Cultural Connections publishes a limited selection of bilingual books and games, and sells culturally authentic artifacts.

Enchanted Lion Books | *www.enchantedlionbooks.com*
A small and fairly young publishing company, Enchanted Lion Books publishes books that "help children to cross all kinds of boundaries and borders." Many of its authors and illustrators are international, although the books are not generally bilingual or dual language. The company also republishes award-winning books from other countries and cultures.

Fitzhenry and Whiteside | *www.fitzhenry.ca/kids.aspx*
A Canadian publisher, Fitzhenry and Whiteside is a source for books about Native and Aboriginal cultures in North America, as well as some titles from other parts of the world.

Groundwood Books | *www.groundwoodbooks.com*
Based in Canada, Groundwood Books has a primary focus on books by and about Canadians, but it also publishes "the stories of people whose voices are not always heard," especially First Nations. The Libros Tigrillo imprint publishes works by people of Latin American origin in both English and Spanish.

HarperCollins/Rayo | *www.harpercollinschildrens.com*

The Rayo imprint publishes "culturally inspired Spanish, English, and bilingual books," as well as translations of award-winning and popular books originally written in English.

Kane/Miller | *www.kanemiller.com*

Kane/Miller publishes award-winning books from around the world. Notably, its online catalog can be searched by the country of origin, and it offers a Libros del Mundo imprint of Spanish-language titles.

Kids Can Press | *www.kidscanpress.com*

Although this Canadian publisher does not currently have books in other languages, many of its multicultural books deal with a global world, and Kids Can Press publishes books based in First Nations Canadian cultures.

Lectura Books | *www.lecturabooks.com*

Lectura Books publishes and distributes a small selection of bilingual books and prides itself on making culturally authentic books available.

Lee and Low | *www.leeandlow.com*

Lee and Low specializes in diversity and publishes books that reflect a variety of cultures. The company makes an effort to work with authors and illustrators of color and is itself a minority-owned company. Its Arcoiris line of books is published in Spanish, but many of its other books are bilingual or dual language. Lee and Low's website also provides high-quality articles that deal with multiculturalism and building literacy in children from non-English-speaking cultures. The site also provides coloring sheets and puzzles.

Live Oak Media | *www.liveoakmedia.com*

Spanish read-along books from this producer add bilingual readings to programs. Kits include bilingual books with readings by professional Hispanic narrators.

Lorito Books | *www.loritobooks.com*

Lorito Books is dedicated to building second-language literacy and an appreciation for the richness of Latino cultures. It provides Spanish and bilingual audiobooks that are culturally relevant and that translate well to the audio format read by native Spanish speakers.

Me + Mi Publishing | *www.memima.com*

Me + Mi is an independent publisher that offers books for infants and toddlers in two or more languages.

Milet Books | *www.milet.com*

This publisher offers books in English and twenty-five other languages, from Albanian to Vietnamese. It also publishes "memory cards" to help children learn languages through educational games.

NorthSouth Books | *www.northsouth.com*
NorthSouth offers many titles in Spanish as translations of popular English-language books, including the Rainbow Fish books by Marcus Pfister, as well as bilingual books.

Pan Asian Publications | *www.panap.com*
The stated mission of this publisher is to promote Chinese cultures and encourage children to learn a second language. Books are adapted from Chinese stories and legends and are available in several Asian languages, including Khmer and Hmong. The publisher also distributes bilingual books in thirty-five languages.

Pangaea | *www.pangaea.org*
This small international publisher offers a few bilingual titles in Spanish for children.

Priddy Books | *http://us.macmillan.com/Priddy.aspx*
Most of this publisher's bilingual titles are board books for very young children that introduce basic concepts in English and Spanish.

Random House | *www.randomhouse.com*
This large publisher has a lengthy list of Spanish-language, dual-language, and bilingual books available. Some are by Hispanic authors, but many are translations of popular titles, like Lucy Cousins's Maisy series.

Raven Tree Press | *www.deltapublishing.com*
Raven Tree Press specializes in children's picture books in English and Spanish as well as bilingual and dual-language books. Books like *Isabel and the Hungry Coyote/ Isabel y el coyote hambriento*, by Keith Polette, look at cross-cultural stories like "Little Red Riding Hood." Activity sheets and programming ideas, such as puppet plays, are provided for many of the books.

Santillana USA | *www.santillanausa.com*
Santillana offers translations of Spanish-language classics and best-selling titles, dual-language books, and authentic literature titles. It also has begun to offer some titles in Haitian Creole.

Shen's Books | *www.shens.com*
Shen's Books publishes titles that emphasize cultural diversity and tolerance. Although its focus is on introducing children to the cultures of Asia, some books reflect multiple cultures.

Star Bright Books | *www.starbrightbooks.com*
Star Bright Books believes "that all children should see themselves in print," and it makes an effort to include children of all colors, nationalities, and abilities in the books it publishes. Some of the books include picture books by Brian Wildsmith and others translated into Arabic, Navajo, Somali, Haitian Creole, and more.

Tricycle Press | *http://tricycle.crownpublishing.com*
Tricycle Press is an imprint of Crown Publishing Group that "creates books that inspire readers to see the world in different ways." It publishes books by Hispanic and Latino authors, like Carmen Tafolla, that are bilingual, as well as books on a global world. Other books, like the World Snacks series, focus on a topic in various cultures and countries.

Tuttle Publishing | *http://peripluspublishinggroup.com/tuttle/*
Tuttle's mission is to publish "books to span the East and West," and its offerings include many favorite stories from Japan, China, India, and other Asian countries.

Distributors and Online Stores

Distributors and online stores carry books from a number of different publishers and can serve as a one-stop shop for many titles. These are a few that specialize in books in languages other than English.

Actrace | *www.chineselibrarysolution.com*
This U.S.-based library service provider specializes in Chinese-language collections, gathering books from a wide selection of publishers. Many titles, including some children's magazines, are in simplified Chinese. Some titles, like *Zen Shorts*, by Jon J. Muth (New York: Scholastic, 2005), have been translated, but many are original Chinese publications.

Amazon (Libros en Español) | *www.amazon.com/Books/b/*
ref=sv_b_5?ie=UTF8&node=301731
This section of the online megabookstore includes "infantil y juvenil" books.

Asia for Kids | *www.afk.com*
This company provides resources, including bilingual books in many Asian and a few non-Asian languages, compiled from a variety of sources. The search function allows you to search for materials by language.

Continental Book Company | *www.continentalbook.com*
A family-owned business, this company is an excellent source for Spanish, bilingual Spanish, French, German, Italian, Arabic, and Chinese publications, including translations of popular and classic children's books.

Independent Publishers Group | *www.ipgbook.com*
This distributor represents many publishers from around the world and offers a variety of children's books in Spanish.

India for Everyone | *www.indiaforeveryone.org*
This distributor offers a wide range of books from India, including bilingual, dual-language, and Hindi books that are original and translations. Notable are some of the graphic novels, translations of Eric Carle's books, and culturally authentic nonfiction titles. Some titles are available in multiple Indian dialects.

Latin American Book Source | *www.latambooks.com*
This distributor states that it can provide any book published in Latin America or Spain.

Lectorum | *www.lectorum.com*
Lectorum is one of the largest distributors of Spanish-language materials in the United States, including works originally written in Spanish and translations from other languages.

Master Communications | *www.master-comm.com*
Although many of the resources focus on Spanish-language materials, this company also supplies sing-and-learn books and CDs for Chinese, Korean, Japanese, and Vietnamese. Special items include bilingual posters that feature words for body parts in six different world languages and activity books. It also resells bilingual children's books and videos that feature family life in other countries.

Pan Asian Publications | *www.panap.com*
A full-service library provider, this company sells books in a number of Asian languages.

Paper Tigers | *www.papertigers.org*
A project of Pacific Rim Voices, this website includes articles, resources, and connections for educators to help promote cross-cultural understanding. Some resources are indexed by country of origin.

Raha Persian Books and Media | *www.rahabooks.com*
Offering Persian and Iranian library materials, selections include bilingual books, music, and film. Some materials are translations, and others are original and culturally authentic.

Russia Online | *http://shop.russia-on-line.com*
This distributor offers books in Russian. Several Dr. Seuss titles are available, along with more authentic children's books.

Skipping Stones | *www.skippingstones.org*

Skipping Stones is a nonprofit magazine for youth that encourages celebration of cultural richness. A typical issue includes poems, stories, articles, and photos from many regions of the United States and the world.

Tsai Fong Books | *www.bookswindow.com*

This distributor sells books in traditional and simplified Chinese, Japanese, Korean, and Vietnamese, as well as audiovisual materials for children and adults.

Websites

Asian/Pacific American Librarians Association | *www.apalaweb.org*

The website for this organization provides background information on various Asian and Pacific American cultures and bibliographies of children's books.

BBC | *www.bbc.co.uk/cbeebies/stories/*

This site from the British Broadcasting Corporation includes online readings of books, some of them in languages other than English. Click on the "World Stories" link to find stories from Turkey, India, Russia, and other countries.

Los Bloguitos | *www.losbloguitos.com*

This Spanish-language blog features children's authors and illustrators and includes stories, tales, poetry, drawings, and more.

**Center for the Study of Books in Spanish
for Children and Adolescents** | *www2.csusm.edu/csb/*

An academic center at the University of California–San Marcos, the center "endeavors to inform current and future educational decision-makers about books centered around Latino people and cultures and about books in Spanish." The website includes an extensive database, in English and Spanish, of recommended books in Spanish, as well as books in English or Spanish about Latinos.

Cody's Cuentos | *www.codyscuentos.com*

This site features a dog and a human pal from Mexico, Spain, or Argentina telling stories each week. A professional storyteller who is also a native speaker performs each podcast.

Colorín Colorado | *www.colorincolorado.org*

This bilingual site for families offers a lot of information and resources that librarians can use with Spanish speakers. Part of the WETA Television project Reading Rockets, the site includes webcasts of interviews with Latino authors and illustrators, as well as guides and tool kits with fabulous resources in English and Spanish.

Criticas | *www.libraryjournal.com/csp/cms/sites/LJ/Reviews/Spanish/*
Formerly a print journal, *Criticas* is now published through *Library Journal* on the Internet. Each month, the journal reviews and archives about two dozen titles for children and young adults.

Cuentos y más | *http://arlington.granicus.com/ViewPublisher.php?view_id=13*
Arlington (Virginia) Public Library produces this television show, also available online, that features stories in Spanish and English. The archived shows are available for free viewing.

International Board on Books for Young People (IBBY) | *www.ibby.org*
This nonprofit organization is a network of people from all over the world who work to bring books and children together. Check the national sections for book lists and information on publishing in a specific country. Also, IBBY sponsors the Hans Christian Andersen Award, which recognizes outstanding authors and illustrators from other countries and their books.

International Children's Digital Library | *http://en.childrenslibrary.org*
The goal of this website is to build a collection of books that represents outstanding historical and contemporary books from around the world. The project aspires to have representation from every culture and language, "so that every child can know and appreciate the riches of children's literature from the world community." Books have been licensed for online distribution, allowing librarians to share books that might otherwise not be readily available. Books are published in the original language, but summaries have been translated into several languages.

Language Lizard | *www.languagelizard.com*
This online retailer provides dual-language books, posters, and CDs in more than forty languages. The "Resources" section also offers articles on language learning and reviews of new titles.

Lee y serás | *www.leeyseras.net*
Created by Scholastic, this site, which translates to "Read and You Will Be," provides information about a program to create print-rich environments for Latino families. The site includes English and Spanish word and reading games and activities, and an online storytime where books are read in Spanish and English.

LitWorld | *http://litworld.org/main.html*
This nonprofit organization works with "vulnerable communities" to support the "development of literacy and the redemptive power of story." The website includes information about the organization's projects and resources that libraries and educators can use to carry out similar programs.

Multicultural Kids | *www.multiculturalkids.com*
This online business offers a variety of items to enhance language learning and cultural and diversity awareness. Dolls, puppets, games, and more that can enhance library programs are available for a number of cultures and languages.

National Writing Project | *www.nwp.org/cs/public/print/resource/2567*
The National Writing Project's *Our Book by Us!/Nuestro libro ¡hecho por nosotros!* is a downloadable template for a bilingual book. Targeted to younger children, each minibook has a story with activity pages that invite readers to add details about their own experiences.

Readers to Eaters | *www.readerstoeaters.com*
The mission of this organization is to connect children and families with food cultures. Cofounded by the publisher Philip Lee, the website provides ideas on ways to use books about food, like *Yum! ¡Mmmm! ¡Qué rico! Americas' Sproutings*, by Pat Mora (New York: Lee and Low, 2007), to appreciate diverse cuisines and cultures.

REFORMA | *www.reforma.org*
This ALA affiliate is an original supporter and founding partner of El día de los niños/El día de los libros, and the website provides information on this celebration and the Mora Award. It also provides information on bilingual programming and materials for youths. A document on promoting bilingual programs also provides translations of a few common phrases related to storytimes and programs.

South Carolina Day-by-Day
Calendar | *www.statelibrary.sc.gov/sc-day-by-day-calendar*
Month by month, day by day, this perpetual calendar offers family literacy activities. The partners in this project also make good partners for Día in your community.

Story Cove | *www.storycove.com*
Sponsored by August House, this website offers video and audio presentations of folktales from around the world. For each folktale, there are also activities and lesson plans.

Storynory | *http://storynory.com*
Free audio stories are provided weekly, including classics and original tales from around the world. The stories come with full English text; double-click on a word for its translation in a variety of different languages.

Tumble Book Library | *www.tumblebooks.com*
This fee-based online database of children's books includes a number of books in languages other than English. Although many titles are offered in Spanish, the collection includes French, Russian, Italian, and Chinese options.

2 Camels | *www.2camels.com*

This website offers a searchable database of festivals that makes it easy and fun to learn about celebrations in other countries and cultures. The database is also searchable by month and includes links to videos and other media showing the celebration.

Librarian's Tool Kits and Manuals for El día de los niños/El día de los libros

Association for Library Service to Children and American Library Association | *www.ala.org/dia/*

The Association for Library Service to Children, a division of the American Library Association, serves as the official "home" for Día. In addition to resources like printable brochures and logos, the site also provides an interactive database of celebrations across the country.

Colorín Colorado | *www.colorincolorado.org/calendar/celebrations/dia*

Developed for Día, this program affiliated with Reading Rockets offers resources for families and activities that libraries and schools can use as part of their celebration. The site also provides webcasts of interviews with bilingual authors.

Día California | *www.diacalifornia.org*

The California State Library's website serves as a Día tool kit, providing tips for successful programming, graphics, and bibliographies.

Día Texas | *www.texasdia.org/toolkit.html*

Developed through a grant from the Kellogg Foundation, this tool kit from the Texas Library Association offers a lot of solid advice and ideas for programming and collection development.

El día de los niños/El día de los libros | *www.tsl.state.tx.us/ld/projects/ninos/*

Texas was the first state to embrace Día, and as part of its commitment, staff at the Texas State Library put together the first manual to help librarians develop their own programs. A Día logo is available for use with any celebration.

National Latino Children's Institute | *www.nlci.org/DLN2004/dlnmain.htm*

Although the emphasis is more on the traditional celebration of Children's Day than on bilingual literacy, the website provides ideas for planning and implementing bilingual programs around April 30.

Pat Mora | *www.patmora.com*

The creator of El día de los niños/El día de los libros hosts a website that provides a wealth of information about the celebration, including Día ideas, a visual history of

Día, and information about programs around the country. Mora's blog *bookjoy* also offers Día "nuggets," compilations of ideas, and other Día information.

Random House | *www.randomhouse.com/kids/pdf/DIA_brochure.pdf*
This publisher's brochure provides several pages of Día ideas and resources, including printable bookmarks for bilingual or Latino books.

Online Manuals for Bilingual and Multicultural Programming

Dígame un cuento/Tell Me a Story: Bilingual Library Programs for Children and Families | *www.tsl.state.tx.us/ld/pubs/bilingual/*
This online manual is a compilation of material from several of the Texas Reading Club manuals organized into one easy-to-use resource guide.

Reading Is Grand | *http://bcalareadingisgrand.weebly.com*
This intergenerational literacy project is presented by the ALA's Black Caucus and targets grandparents raising their grandchildren.

Talk Story Together | *www.talkstorytogether.org/libraries*
This project from the American Indian Library Association and the Asian/Pacific American Librarians Association provides material to strengthen local communities through the enjoyment of reading books, hearing stories, and connecting to ethnicity and culture.

Texas Reading Club | *www.tsl.state.tx.us/ld/projects/trc/*
Each year, the Texas State Library develops manuals for library summer-reading clubs and makes the manual available to all online. Each manual includes bilingual programming that can be used throughout the year as part of a Día celebration.

Mora Award

Pat Mora and her family established the Estela and Raúl Mora Award in 2000 to honor their parents, who instilled in their children a love of reading, and to motivate libraries to celebrate El día de los niños/El día de los libros. Members of REFORMA, the National Association to Promote Library and Information Services to Latinos and the Spanish-Speaking, serve as judges for the award, which consists of a check for $1,000 and a plaque donated by the Mora grandchildren. The award may be granted to a public library or school or an organization working with either a library or school as the sponsor for El día de los niños/El día de los libros. To submit your program for this award, visit the REFORMA website (www.reforma .org/Mora2010.htm) for the application. Applications are generally due in mid-August for programs presented during the previous year.

2000 Award: Austin (Texas) Public Library

2001 Award: El Paso (Texas) Public Library

2002 Award: Multnomah County (Oregon) Library

2003 Award: Corvallis-Benton County (Oregon) Public Library

2004 Award: Providence (Rhode Island) Public Library

2005 Award: REFORMA de Utah

2006 Award: Kenton County (Kentucky) Public Library

2007 Award: Broward County (Florida) Public Library

2008 Award: Public Library of Charlotte and Mecklenburg County (North Carolina) and Riverside County (California) Library System

2009 Award: Topeka and Shawnee County (Kansas) Public Library and San Francisco Public Library

2010 Award: Arthur F. Turner Community Library of Yolo County, West Sacramento (California); Pima County Public Library, Tucson (Arizona); and Santa Barbara Public Library System, Santa Barbara (California)

Bibliography

Alexander, Linda B., and Nahyun Kwon. *Multicultural Programs for Tweens and Teens.* Chicago: American Library Association, 2010.

Alire, Camila. "President's Message—Advocacy: Part II." *American Libraries* online, October 23, 2009, http://americanlibrariesmagazine.org/columns/presidents -message/advocacy-part-ii.

Balderrama, Sandra Rios. "Serving Multicultural Populations by Increasing Our Cross-Cultural Awareness in Libraries: Japan and the USA Serving Latin Americans, Brazilians, Latinos and Hispanics," Current Awareness Portal, http://current.ndl.go.jp/node/14412 (accessed December 11, 2010).

Blass, Rosanne. *Windows on the World.* Santa Barbara, CA: Libraries Unlimited, 2010.

Crandall, Hope, Mary Parra, and Deeda Chamberlain. "Community Collaborates for a Día Celebration." *OLA Quarterly* 5 (Winter 2009): 25–27.

East, Kathy, and Rebecca L. Thomas. *Across Cultures: A Guide to Multicultural Literature for Children.* Westport, CT: Libraries Unlimited, 2007.

Elturk, Ghada. "Diversity and Cultural Competency." *Colorado Libraries* 29 (Winter 2003): 5–7.

"English Won't Dominate as World Language." MSNBC, February 26, 2004, www .msnbc.msn.com/id/4387421.

Forzani, Anneke. "The Multicultural Library: How Librarians Are Responding to the Needs of Ethnically Diverse Communities." Language Lizard, 2007, www .languagelizard.com/v/vspfiles/newsarticle8.htm.

Gandini, Lella, and Simonetta Sambrotta. "Italian Nursery Rhymes: A Rich, Varied, and Well-Used Landscape," *Lion and the Unicorn* 26 (April 2002): 203–22.

Ghoting, Saroj Nadkarni, and Pamela Martin-Díaz. *Early Literacy Storytimes @ your library.* Chicago: American Library Association, 2006.

Howrey, Sara P. "*De colores*: The Universal Language of Bilingual Storytime." *American Libraries* 34 (October 2003): 38–43.

Jeffers, Dawn. "Bilingual Books for ESL Students . . . and Beyond." *Children and Libraries* 7 (Winter 2009): 38–39.

King, Mark A., Anthony Sims, and David Osher. "How Is Cultural Competency Integrated into Education?" Center for Effective Collaboration and Practice, [2007?], http://cecp.air.org/cultural/Q_integrated.htm.

Kuglin, Mandee. "Latino Outreach: Making Día a Fiesta of Family Literacy." *Children and Libraries* 7 (Winter 2009): 42–46.

Kuharets, Olga R. *Venture into Cultures: A Resource Book of Multicultural Materials and Programs.* Chicago: American Library Association, 2001.

Larson, Jeanette, and Rose Zertuche Treviño. *Color Your World . . . Read! 2004 Texas Reading Club Manual.* Austin: Texas State Library and Archives Commission, Library Development Division, 2004.

Marquis, Solina Kasten. "Collections and Services for the Spanish-Speaking: Issues and Resources." *Public Libraries* 42 (March–April 2003): 106–12.

Mora, Pat. *Book Fiesta! Celebrate Children's Day/Book Day / Celebremos El día de los niños/El día de los libros.* New York: HarperCollins, 2009.

———. *Tomás and the Library Lady.* New York: Alfred A. Knopf, 1997.

———. *Zing! Seven Creativity Practices for Educators and Students.* Thousand Oaks, CA: Corwin Press, 2010.

Mora, Pat, and Rose Zertuche Treviño. "Celebrating Children and Books." *Book Links* 17 (January–February 2007): 24–25.

Overall, Patricia Montiel. "Cultural Competence: A Conceptual Framework for Library and Information Science Professionals." *Library Quarterly* 79 (April 2009): 175–204.

Roy, Loriene. "Let Book Joy Begin @ your library! Ten Years of El día de los niños/ El día de los libros." *Library Media Connection* 25 (March 2007): 14–16.

Totten, Herman, et al. *Culturally Diverse Library Collections for Youth.* New York: Neal-Schuman Publishers, 1996.

Van Dusen, Melissa. "Open Up with Community Outreach." *Library Media Connection* 25 (March 2007): 24–26.

Wadham, Tim. *Libros esenciales: Building, Marketing, and Programming a Core Collection of Spanish Language Children's Materials.* New York: Neal-Schuman Publishers, 2007.

Index

Note: Italicized page numbers indicate illustrations.

You may also be interested in

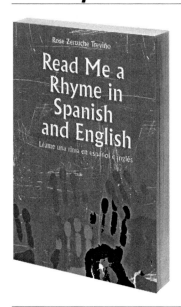

READ ME A RHYME IN SPANISH AND ENGLISH

Rose Zertuche Treviño

"Full of rhymes, songs and finger plays in English and Spanish, this book is ideal for programs serving dual language learners."—*Teaching Young Children*

"Librarians who follow Treviño's recommendations can not only present successful bilingual storytimes, but also fulfill the educational and recreational needs of Latino parents and children who are trying to adjust themselves to a different culture."—*School Library Journal*

ISBN: 978-0-8389-0982-9
160 PAGES / 6" x 9"

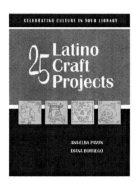

Order today at **alastore.ala.org** or **866-746-7252!**

ALA Store purchases fund advocacy, awareness, and accreditation programs for library professionals worldwide.

CPSIA information can be obtained at www.ICGtesting.com
Printed in the USA
LVOW021651111211

258899LV00005B/7/P

9 780838 935996